UNDERSTANDING
THE MINI PROPHETS

MALCOLM HEDDING

UNDERSTANDING THE MINI PROPHETS

MALCOLM HEDDING

ISBN 978-0-9890173-7-4

Published by:
Main Street Books
Memphis, TN

Printed in USA by The Print Steward.
Grand Rapids, MI

This book is dedicated to the Assemblies of God of Southern Africa; one of the great Pentecostal movements of our time.

Contents

The Mini Prophets

It is both usual and normal for Bible teachers to refer to that body of prophetic literature in the Old Testament as Major and Minor Prophets. A Major Prophet would be Isaiah or Jeremiah and Ezekiel and a Minor Prophet would be the likes of Joel, Amos, Hosea, and Zechariah etc. However, there are some Minor Prophets in this group that can be called Mini Prophets as their prophetic oracles, while very powerful, are also very short; no more than a chapter or three. I recently undertook a tour of ministry to Finland and upon praying about what I should teach on the Holy Spirit clearly led me to the Mini Prophets and so consequently, night after night, I expounded on another Mini Prophet. The blessing of God upon this was obvious and surprising and the material I handled startled me as I suddenly saw a pattern in all of them that made clear the purpose of God for the days in which we live. I have been so impacted by this phenomenon that I have now decided to write a book about it called:

Understanding the Mini Prophets

So, here it is and it is my prayer that you will be impacted as I have and that this will change your way of living as it certainly has mine. We live in the most amazing times and indeed the most dangerous. The Church everywhere is under the judgment of God and will be refined. God always begins with us first and then He will turn in earnest to the world. We are about to witness things that we have never seen before and consequently the hearts of many will begin to tremble and fail them. Even the elect will be tempted to embrace deception and the Middle East will boil and trouble the world without remedy.

The Mini Prophets hold a very important message for us and we should learn it well and so I would strongly urge you to read them first before reading this book. Also be sure to keep your Bible open at the passage being referred to as you read this short work. This is very important and again I strongly urge you to do it. This volume will then take a look at Zephaniah, Haggai, Obadiah, Habakkuk, Nahum and Joel. Let us then brace ourselves and begin the journey.

With every blessing,

Malcolm Hedding
Murfreesboro Tennessee
2017

Foreword

Malcolm Hedding's books are grounded in practical theology. Over the many years that I have known him, his teachings and writings leave you with the theological and philosophical question "How then should we live?"

Using the interesting title *"The Mini Prophets"*, Malcolm reviews the brief oracles of six Minor Prophets. Crossing the hermeneutical bridge from there and then, to here and now, Malcolm exhorts the believer today to be aware of not committing the same sins that took Israel into exile. This is a challenge against shallow worship, the approaching Day of the Lord and the minimizing of sin. In contrast the exhortation is for prayerful, powerful seeking of the Lord and His Kingdom, manifest in mercy and righteous living.

Using Israel, Jerusalem and the Temple as types and shadows of the ultimate reality found in the Messiah, Malcolm writes about the lateness of the hour and the complacency of the Church in the West. A modern expression is a *"normalcy bias"*. This term means that when people are facing impending disaster, they deny, dismiss or diminish any possibility of danger. The Mini Prophets remind us to awake unto righteousness for the day is ending, and the night is at hand.

Dr. David Elms
Founding Minister of Kingsway Christian Fellowship, Liverpool
United Kingdom Director of the International Christian Embassy
Jerusalem

ZEPHANIAH

**"The Lord your God in your midst,
the Mighty One, will save; He will
rejoice over you with gladness, He
will quiet you in His love, He will
rejoice over you with singing."**
Zephaniah 3:17

Here's a prophet who was called to give his prophetic oracle round about 600 BC, when Judah was outwardly undergoing a revival. Zephaniah was a pre-exilic prophet and his ministry took place at the time when a godly king called Josiah was introducing spiritual reforms to bring the nation back to God. That, which sparked this revival, if we can call it that, was the discovery of a copy of the Law of Moses in the Temple. Upon hearing its message Josiah repented and called for a renewal of spiritual and moral life in the nation. One can read all about this in 2 Chronicles 34-35. Apparently this renewal was only "skin deep" and so Zephaniah arrives on the scene to lay bare the weakness of the movement. His words are clear and challenging and we are therefore reminded that true revival is more than outward form and huge numbers flocking to the house of God. No it must begin with the heart which must be refocused to obey God through repentance and holy living. The word of God must therefore pierce like a sword and those who preach it must ensure that it does even if it angers people.

So, as we look at this mini prophet let us do so with a heart that hears his message and seeks to obey it. The book of Zephaniah, like all the other prophetic books of the Bible, transcends time and speaks to us today. The contents of the book, for our purposes, may be understood in the following way:

Concepts

Israel is the 'platform" from which the purpose of God has arisen and flowed out into the nations. She is thus in a place of privilege and God holds her accountable for the light that she has received. In blessing the world, as God first declared to Abraham, Israel is required to be an example of the treasure that God has deposited in her. Consequently the nations round about her are also held accountable. Sadly Israel has abandoned her calling, the nations have loved wickedness and God warns Israel and the nations that great judgment is coming. This terrifying judgment finds expression in the coming Day of the Lord. It will begin in Judah at the very temple of God!

> **"I will stretch out My hand against Judah, and against all the inhabitants of Jerusalem. I will cut off every trace of Baal from this place, the names of the idolatrous priests with the pagan priests-Those who worship the host of heaven on the housetops; those who worship and swear oaths by the Lord, but who also swear by Milcom; those who have turned back from following the Lord, and have not sought the Lord, nor enquired of Him." "Be silent in the presence of the Lord; for the day of the Lord is at hand, for the Lord has prepared a sacrifice; He has invited His guests."**
> **Zephaniah 1:4-7**

Judgment always begins at the house of God because the city cannot be cleaned up until the house of God is cleaned up (*1 Peter 4:17*). Jesus demonstrated this principle when, having entered Jerusalem triumphantly He cleaned up the Temple and not the city by getting rid of the Romans. Consequently the masses were disappointed and enraged and for one person called Judas this was the "last straw" and so he determined to betray Jesus and did. Today, the Church, though in many places still strong and faithful, is increasingly departing from the ways of God just as Judah did and much of it is becoming a reflection of the world around it and not of Christ. Scripture warns us that the end-time church will be a spiritual harlot and that this would be one of the signs of the approaching great Day of the Lord.

> **"So he carried me away in the Spirit into the wilderness. And I saw a woman sitting on a scarlet beast which**

was full of names of blasphemy, having seven heads and ten horns. The woman was arrayed in purple and scarlet, and adorned with gold and precious stones and pearls, full of abominations and the filthiness of her fornication. And on her forehead a name was written:

**MYSTERY,
BABYLON THE GREAT
THE MOTHER OF HARLOTS
AND OF THE ABOMINATIONS OF THE EARTH.**

I saw the woman, drunk with the blood of the saints and with the blood of the martyrs of Jesus. And when I saw her I marveled with great amazement."

Revelation 17:3-6

The Day of the Lord is immediate, progressive and final. That is, it comes in present judgment as it did in 586 BC when the city of Jerusalem was finally ransacked and destroyed by the Babylonians. It also came again in 70 AD when the same thing happened on exactly the same day, the 9th day of Av, nearly 700 years later. It also came time and time again in history when nations were overthrown by God and the Church was persecuted and scattered and it also came in the Second World War when mayhem and destruction rained down on much of Europe and England. However, there is a final Great Day of the Lord that is fast approaching when all nations will be judged, including Israel. The Church too will be laid bare for all to see her nakedness and blindness and Jesus warned of this in His revelation to John (*Revelation 3:17*). Zephaniah's warning is therefore clear and sobering! As for the final Great Day of the Lord he writes:

"The great day of the Lord is near; it is near and hastens quickly. The noise of the day is bitter; there the mighty men shall cry out. That day is a day of wrath, a day of trouble and distress, a day of devastation and desolation, a day of clouds and thick darkness, a day of trumpet and alarm against the fortified cities and against the high towers. I will bring distress upon men, and they shall walk like blind men, because they have sinned against the Lord; their blood shall be poured out like dust and their flesh like refuse."

Zephaniah 1:14-17

It is clear from this passage that this Day of the Lord is more than just regional judgment against Israel and the nations but a terrifying judgment against all nations. It looms like a shadow over all nations and peoples because they have rejected God and sinned against Him. This concept of a "greater day of judgment within a day" is found in all of scripture. We should note this and quite frankly wake up because it is coming our way today. So;

1. All the prophets speak of it *(Isaiah 2:10-21; Jeremiah 25:30-33; Ezekiel:10-19; Malachi 4:1-3; Zechariah 14; Obadiah 15-16; Joel 3:14-16; Haggai 2:20-22)*
2. Jesus warned about it *(Matthew 24:21)*
3. John the Baptist referred to it *(Luke 3:7)*
4. Paul wrote about it *(1 Thessalonians 5:1-5)*
5. Peter informs the church about it *(Acts 2:17-21; 2 Peter 3:7; 10-12)*...and,
6. John describes it. (Revelation 14:17-20)

In short we have been warned and yet hardly anyone preaches about it today! It presently rages through the Middle East and Africa and consequently thousands of Christians are being martyred. It will cover the world and it is fast approaching. We should heed Zephaniah's warning.

Requirements

Josiah's reformation was sincere and genuine but it lacked spiritual depth. God is looking for repentance, a heart change and restitution. That is, behavior that is consistent with repentance and this repentance is characterized by godly sorrow that in turn delights in the ways of God *(1Corinthians 7:9)*. So, true revival begins with what Paul calls the "inner man." The lack of this needed a prophet to pinpoint the failures of Josiah's reformation. The lesson is clear; we can easily mistake revival for outward forms of religiosity but God looks on the heart. Much of what has been termed revival in recent years has simply in the end been just another Christian fad! Revival will come when preachers are prepared again to wield the word of God as a sword with the clear intention of wounding the heart. The writer of the book of Hebrews states:

> **"For the word of God is living and powerful, and sharper than any two-edged sword, piercing even to**

the division of soul and spirit, and is a discerner of the
thoughts and intents of the heart."

Hebrews 4:12

Today sin is never defined and explained; it is merely mentioned as "sin" which in reality is a generic term which gives a broad definition only to what displeases God. By contrast, though Paul clearly uses the word sin in his letters, he frequently gives us an in depth analysis of what it really amounts to. This never happens today and consequently the results are lacking. So, here is just one list of human pursuits that Paul labels as sin:

"Now the works of the flesh are evident, which are:
adultery, fornication, uncleanness, lewdness, idolatry,
jealousies, outbursts of wrath, selfish ambitions,
dissensions, heresies, envy, murders, drunkenness,
revelries and the like; of which I tell you beforehand,
just as I also told you in time past, that those who
practice such things will not inherit the kingdom of
God."   **Galatians 5:19-21**

Note also: 1 Corinthians 6:9-11 and Romans 1:28-32
God then speaking through Zephaniah calls upon a heart response from His people and therefore He desires that they should:

1. Seek Him *(1:6)*. Jesus said that the Temple of God should be a house of prayer for all nations *(Matthew 21:13)*. The Church is the Temple of God *(Ephesians 2:19-22)* and therefore its major activity should be that of prayer; but it is not. It is rather a house of preaching, teaching, singing and even entertainment but definitely not a house of prayer. Today not even ten percent of local congregations gather together for corporate prayer and then we wonder why evil marches on unopposed in our streets and why our influence in the world is so weak. It is because we do not seek God!

2. Be enthusiastic and zealous for the things of God *(1:12)*. God hates lukewarm Christians! Here we are told that He uses a lamp to

search out the faithful believers but those that are complacent and lukewarm He will punish. This indeed is picked up by Jesus in His Revelation to John where He declares that lukewarm Christians will be vomited out of His mouth (*Revelation 3:16*). The image He presents here is disgusting or gross, as a teenager would say, but it is deliberate because He wishes to convey His displeasure at complacent Christianity. True revival will change this.

3. Be reverent in His house (*1:9*). The Church of Jesus has a great dignity in that it is the Temple of the Holy Spirit (*Ephesians 2:19-22*).Today we have far too many so called Christian Centers. Consequently, people attend meetings and become "meeting connoisseurs"! They will even sit in the meeting quietly checking their emails or Facebook status without any shame or sense of embarrassment. They are thus "leaping over the threshold", treating God and His people with irreverence and disrespect and thereby inviting His displeasure. By contrast God says, "Be silent in the presence of the Lord...." (*1:7*).

4. Be merciful and meek (*2:3*). This is a wonderful exhortation because firstly it is given to all peoples and essentially calls the listener to be humble of heart and mind; to be mindful of those who need help and deliverance from the strong and secondly; because it calls us to seek righteousness. Righteousness is the very nature of God and through Christ's finished work on the cross, we receive it as a gift (*it is imputed*) and we appropriate it (*it is imparted*) by on going faith. A true move of God will induce a thirst for God's nature and ways. Holiness is a term that the modern church knows very little of and certainly one does not hear it preached from the average pulpit and yet without it we shall not see the Lord (*Hebrews 12:14*).

True revival must have all these components in it and so the Prophet Zephaniah calls his people to account and all the time, in the background, the sword of the Lord is about to fall, not in blessing, but in judgment because the people of God will just not change their ways. I feel ,in the Spirit of God, that days of great upheaval are now just before us since much of the church in the West is complacent, given to compromise and at ease. The people of God are sleeping, their ears are being tickled from many a pulpit (*2 Timothy 4:3*) and meaningful corporate prayer has been abandoned. The Day of the Lord is at hand!

Warnings

Zephaniah, having addressed the weaknesses of the reformation in Judah, now turns his attention on the nations round about. Gaza, Moab, Ethiopia and Assyria are all called to account *(2:4-19)*. Mostly these nations are judged because of their abuse of Israel. They have despised Israel; they have threatened Israel; they have arrogantly dealt with Israel and have sought to disinvest Israel of her borders. Sounds a lot like today! God will bring them down and in the past did. However, the prophet "skips forward to the future" even beyond our time and tells us that a day is coming when:

> **"The Lord will be awesome to them, for He will reduce to nothing all the gods of the earth; people shall worship Him, each one from his place, indeed all the shores of the nations."** **Zephaniah 2:11**

This is a warning of global judgment in the future with the promise that the people of Israel will be restored and revived truly in a way that all nations will abandon their gods and only worship the God of Israel. So, once again, the "smaller judgment" of Zephaniah's day is eclipsed by a global judgment that will vindicate Israel on a global scale. This is surely coming even though all the nations of the earth rage against Israel today. Zephaniah's oracle is a warning to them…and indeed to the wider church that so easily sets out to boycott, sanction and condemn Israel today. God is watching, waiting and will make His move in due course in that He will "stretch out His hand" and judge them *(2:13)*.

Endings

The final chapter of this remarkable little book focuses on the spiritual failure of Judah/Jerusalem in spite of the fact that God faithfully reached out to her morning by morning with His love and faithfulness *(3:5)*. Apostasy has gripped prophet and priest and trickled down to the people. God even judged other nations around her in an attempt to awaken His people spiritually *(3:6-7)*. All to no avail; the revival is not going well. Israel will thus be judged and exiled and this is the testimony of history but it is not the end of the story for God promises an amazing day of restoration. True revival bringing remarkable blessing to Israel is on its way. So then, what will God's endings look like?

1. To soften Israel spiritually and lead her to repentance He will gather all nations against her *(3:8)*. In so doing He will also judge them for their wickedness and make a complete end of them but Israel will be saved *(Jeremiah 30:11)*. Zechariah also spoke of this coming conflict and he put it this way in the twelfth chapter of his oracle, "Behold, I will make Jerusalem a cup of drunkenness to all the surrounding peoples, when they lay siege against Judah and Jerusalem. And it shall happen in that day that I will make Jerusalem a very heavy stone for all peoples; all who would heave it away will surely be cut in pieces, though all nations of the earth are gathered against it" *(Zechariah 12:2-2)*. Israel's resistance against Jesus, sadly stiffened by Christian anti-Semitism through the centuries, is strong and certain. This means that only God can remove it and He will. It will be a painful process to watch but it will happen and Paul confirmed it in his letter to the Roman Church *(Romans 11:25-26)*.

2. This huge conflict in the Middle East, embracing all the nations of the earth, will thus drive Israel to her God and so true revival will break out and the first confirming sign of this will be the language of repentance and calling out to the Lord *(3:9)*. Consequently Israel will serve her Lord Messiah and certainly, as we watch events unfolding before us in the Middle East, we can clearly observe "the gathering storm." Zephaniah is truly a prophet for our time.

3. The victory that God will give Israel at every level, and mainly at that of the spiritual, will surprise her, humble her before God and lead to another great Aliyah; this time from "beyond the rivers of Ethiopia" *(3:10-11)*.

4. Israel will be soundly converted to Messiah and will be at rest but most of all she will be filled with joy, amazement and singing because her Messiah King will be in her midst dwelling with her *(3:14-15)*. This day is soon coming and it will bring to Israel a blessing and peacefulness that she has not known since God first called her into being some four thousand years ago when He encountered Abraham. This reigning King will be none other than Jesus of Nazareth *(3:16)*. Indeed we have here a marvelous picture of Messiah God singing and rejoicing over His people. A people that will include believers from every nation and tribe that have joined with Israel in her great redemptive Olive Tree *(Romans 11:17-22)*. In fact we

learn from this that God has surprising emotions because He will sing and rejoice over the redeemed of Zion *(3:17)*.

5. Israel will enjoy fame and praise in all the earth. The great work of Aliyah today is a foreshadowing of all these good things to come *(3:18-20)*.

These are the "endings" that God, by the words of Zephaniah, assures us of. The vision will not fail and so what is weak and inadequate in Josiah's reformation will finally be corrected and replaced with true revival. Blessed be the God of Israel who calls us to know and pray for these things. Here ends the oracle of Zephaniah.

DEVOTION

Israel, the Church and the Nations

"I have lived, Sir, a long time and the longer I live the more convincing proofs I see of this truth, that God governs in the affairs of men. And if a sparrow cannot fall to the ground without His notice, is it probable an empire can rise without His aid? We have been assured Sir, in the Sacred Writings, that "except the Lord build the House, they labor in vain who build it." I firmly believe this, and I also believe that without His concurring aid we shall succeed in this political building no better than the builders of Babel. We shall be divided by our partial local interests; our projects will be confounded, and we ourselves shall become a reproach and bye word down to future ages. And what is worse, mankind may hereafter from this unfortunate instance, despair of establishing governments by human wisdom and leave it to chance, war and conquest."

"I therefore beg leave to move that henceforth prayers imploring the assistance of Heaven, and its blessings on our deliberations be held in this Assembly every morning before we proceed to business, and that one or more of the clergy of the city be requested to officiate in that service."

James Madison 1787

The sovereignty of God

As we journey through this world we must be reminded more than ever that the God of the Bible exercises continuing power and sovereignty over the nations. The message of the Mini Prophets certainly highlights this as the God we serve deals with Israel, the nations and those who love and know Him. He has not abandoned the world to the forces of chaos and evil. Though He may "shake them", and He is, He is still in control of all things, in heaven and on earth. Isaiah, in his great prophetic oracle, saw the nations as God saw them and consequently understood that they were but a drop in a bucket of water *(Isaiah 40:15-17)*. We can sometimes be overwhelmed by their rage and power but God simply uses them to advance His will and purpose in the world and then, once this is accomplished, He blows them away like chaff in the wind *(Daniel 2:35)*.

The truth is, a new global kingdom is coming and it's coming through a Jewish Jerusalem! It will be a kingdom of righteousness and peace and so war will be a thing of the past; the nations will learn war no more. This kingdom will replace all the great gentile kingdoms and it will be the "kingdom of our Lord and of His Christ" *(Revelation 11:15)*. It will never be vanquished and preparations for its coming are now observed in the modern day restoration of Israel. However, its coming will be preceded by the arrival of the great and terrible Day of the Lord and we are presently witnessing the preparations for this coming Day in the nations *(Acts 2:20; 2Peter 3:10; Revelation 6:12-17)*. Wickedness, rebellion against the God of the Bible, the rejection of authority and the loathing of Israel is everywhere accompanied with moral depravity and rage on the streets of our cities. We live in perilous times! *(2 Timothy 3:1-5)*

The Church in crisis

Even the Church in its visible, historical institutional form is departing from the "faith which was once for all delivered to the saints" *(Jude 3)*; and is not only therefore embracing error but actually applauding those who do so *(Romans 1:32)*. A great apostasy is upon us and this in itself is deceptive because the Church appears to be growing but it is not doing so in truth! The teachings of "another Christ" are penetrating the church at all levels. The coming Great Day of God Almighty will lay waste the spiritual bankruptcy of the Church and it will humble the world with its false gods and love of money and power *(Revelation 18)*. The true follower of Christ is called to come out of the world and this apostate Church *(Revelation 18:4)*. The Day of the Lord will see Israel delivered and saved; the true Church resurrected and glorified and the Son of God seated on His glorious throne in Zion *(Psalm 2)*. These glorious truths embolden the followers of Jesus to seek to hasten the coming of the Day of the Lord *(2 Peter 3:10-13)*, all the while holding out to "the whosoever will" the word of life.

Israel at the crossroads

Israel, though strong, has, by the misguided policies of its political leadership, made itself vulnerable and weak. The failure to win wars in the last two decades coupled with her acceptance of the notion of occupation and that of a two state solution has "boxed her in" politically because she is now honor bound to keep her promises to the international community. This is something, in reality, that she cannot do because, if she did, she will commit national suicide! Her interlocker is not a peace partner but a war maker and it has skillfully used the so called peace process to win concessions from her that compound her defensive needs and set her up for the kill. The withdrawal from Gaza in 2005 was heralded as an act of peace whereas it was in reality an act of stupidity. Since then thousands of rockets have rained down on Israel's cities and there are more to come.

None of this should have ever happened because the San Remo Agreement of 1922, verified by the League of Nations, affirmed that Israel's land would include all the land west of the Jordan River. This agreement was fully endorsed and verified by the United Nations in 1948. This means that the San Remo Agreement of 1922 and 1948 is a binding resolution of the United Nations and as such was a reflection of the will of the international community. Israel's failure to assert this agreement has brought her to the cul-de-sac in which she now finds herself. The Madrid peace conference, followed by the Oslo Accords, the Philadelphian Process and all the recent peace conferences weakened Israel's position because she de facto surrendered her rights protected under the San Remo Agreement. In the meantime, Israel's perceived failure to abandon the occupation and set up a two state solution has inflamed anti-Semitism in Europe and has encouraged the western democracies to slowly move toward unilateralism. Hence nation after nation in Europe is recognizing the existence of a Palestinian State with Jerusalem as its capital. To be honest, Israel's place in the world is becoming precarious and so Jerusalem is fast becoming what the Bible calls, a heavy stone to lift (*Zechariah 12:2-3*).

As I write Hamas has rearmed and continues to hold an arsenal of some 30,000 missiles; to the north Hezbollah is entrenched on Israel's border and has under its control some 50,000 missiles and to the east; Iran is racing towards the acquisition of a nuclear weapon. The ever weak and gullible West has been "strung along" by the cunning intrigue of the Mullahs thus buying Iran the time she needs to get to the point where she can "make the end dash" to nuclear capability. So, the options for Israel are: If she success-fully destroys her enemies she will incur the wrath of the world; on the other hand, if she negotiates a two state solution she will be committing national suicide and; if she does nothing she will be embroiled in a never ending war; a war that the international community will be reluctant to get involved with because of their huge Muslim populations in their own backyards. Israel needs a "miracle politician" and sadly she may just get one!

According to the Bible, and I do fully trust it, Israel will be brought to near ruin and then God will step in and deliver her (*Zechariah 12:1-9*) and at the same time make a full end of the nations (*Jeremiah 30:11*). Israel is destined for great glory but this only after she has been humbled and delivered by her Messiah. This constitutes the nature of the conflict unfolding day by day before us now.

The new emerging world powers

On another front we are sadly witnessing the decline of America and the rise of Russia and China. America is presently crippled by an ever-rising 19 trillion dollar debt problem while China, which also holds a considerable amount of America's debt, holds a 40 trillion dollar reserve. Senator Ted Cruz, and indeed others, has said that America's biggest national security threat is its debt. This is true. So then, while the international community recently placed sanctions on the Russian economy for that country's military adventures in Crimea and the Ukraine, China quietly bailed out Putin to blunt these sanctions and thereby to forge a stronger Sino/Russian alliance. Both nations are investing heavily in rearmament while the USA, by contrast, has in recent years slashed its defense budget and thereby compromising its capability to fight on two fronts simultaneously. New, and might I add, totalitarian, powers are arising and, according to the Bible, these powers will play a huge and crucial role in the Middle East *(Revelation 16:12-16; Ezekiel 39:1-4)*. We should be watching and praying as never before.

Lance Lambert

Finally, I wish to write a few words about Lance Lambert who passed away on the 10th May 2015. I first met Lance in the early eighties and from that time forward we became firm and close friends. We preached together throughout South Africa and beyond and in every way he was a unique gift to the Body of Christ, a remarkable and eloquent Bible teacher and a prophet to the Church of Jesus Christ. Lance was part of the founding group of the International Christian Embassy Jerusalem and in his heart were always the "highways to Zion." He lived out what he preached and his ministry, spanning many decades, was undergirded by his relentless commitment to prayer and intercession. I well remember attending his weekly prayer meetings that he held in his home in Jerusalem in the suburb of Yemen Moshe'. They were focused, supported by scripture, which he truly used as a sword, and so they were also powerful. Lance knew how to pray and believed that prayer was "caught" and not taught. We caught it in his home!

Lance leaves a huge gap in our lives and yet we know that he finished his personal race and has therefore completed all the work that Jesus called him to do. Like Daniel, he will now rise in the resurrection of the righteous to assume the eternal place allotted to him. We thank God for his life and ministry and recognize that his words will still speak to us through the written and spoken legacy that he left us.

Our appropriate response

So, dear friends, given all of the above what sort of people should we be? The answer is in Hebrews 12: 1-2:

"Therefore we also, since we are surrounded by so great a cloud of witnesses; let us lay aside every weight, and the sin which so easily ensnares us, and let us run with endurance the race that is set before us, looking unto Jesus, the author and finisher of our faith, who for the joy that was set before Him endured the cross, despising the shame, and has sat down at the right hand of the throne of God."

The writer tells us that we should:

1. Recognize that millions of people have walked with God, through thick and thin, and have now taken the glorious seat of an Overcomer in God's great pavilion. We must determine to follow them.

2. Lay aside every "weight" or "encumbrance", as another translation puts it. A "weight" is something quite legitimate but not helpful as it takes up too much time, energy and resources that could be better employed in the cause of Christ.

3. Lay aside every sin that ensnares us. Sin, not dealt with displeases God as it is a contradiction of Who He is. We must keep short accounts with sin and not think, for a moment, that we can play with it and retain healthy spiritual lives (*1 John 1:8-9*).

4. Look unto Jesus for He is the author and finisher of our faith. This means that our relationship with Him must be real and powerful. Anything short of this is just the mechanics of religion even if it is Christian by appearance.

5. Run with endurance being filled with joy. We have much work to do and little time to do it in. Our work is to make Christ known by our words and character; that is, we must walk the talk! We must also arm ourselves against hardship and spiritual attack and we must stand with and pray for Israel.

Even so, Lord Jesus come and come quickly!

HAGGAI

**""I will shake heaven and earth. I will
overthrow the throne of kingdoms;
I will destroy the strength of the
Gentile kingdoms".**

Haggai 2:22

Haggai is a restoration Prophet because his oracle is given after the return
of the Jews from Babylon at about 500 BC. We are told at the beginning of
the book that Zerubbabel was the Governor and Jehozadak was the High
Priest. By this time the first wave of returning Jews had taken place some
twenty years before and so the city was indeed rebuilt, its walls were repaired
but the House of the Lord remained in disrepair. Thus life had stabilized,
commerce and trade were flourishing and some of the people were living in
paneled homes. The good old days were back and prosperity had blunted the
spiritual vision of the people, much like it has today! God was not pleased
because His goodness had been taken for granted, a fact demonstrated by
the poor state of His House. Haggai is thus commissioned by God to awaken
His people to some spiritual realities and truths *(1:1-2)*. His prophecy then
asserts that:

The Kingdom of God was being neglected *(1:2-6)*

> **"Is it time for you yourselves to dwell in your paneled
> houses, and the temple to lie in ruins."**

Haggai 1:4

The Kingdom of God can be defined as the place where God is present and has His way. In Haggai's time God was present in His temple in Jerusalem and indeed the temple site is the place where He has put His name and presence forever. Those who lived and worshipped there were expected to approach Him by atonement, love Him with all their hearts and live for Him *(Psalm 48:12-14; Psalm 132:13-14)*. The sad truth is that having gotten established again, after the exile, they quickly forgot God, were doing their own thing and had left His house in ruins. Consequently God calls them through the Prophet to consider their ways *(1:5)*.

This word is as applicable today as it was two thousand five hundred years ago. The Temple of God is now His local Church and for too many Christians the house of God is not a priority. It is certainly important but not the chief concern of their lives. The truth is, Jesus is not Lord of their lives and He cannot get them to change their ways. Scripture teaches us that we are to seek first the Kingdom of God, that we must do what Jesus says and that we must live as He wants us to *(Luke 6:46; Matthew 7:21-23)*.

> **"But seek first the kingdom of God and His righteousness, and all these things shall be added to you."**
> **Matthew 6:33**

Indeed, God loves His people so much that He endeavors to impact their ears by reminding them that it does not go well with them when they neglect His House:

> **"You have sown much and bring in little; you eat, but do not have enough; you drink, but you are not filled with drink; you clothe yourselves, but no one is warm; and he who earns wages, earns wages to put into a bag of holes."**
> **Haggai 1:6**

We are created to love God and serve Him and so when He occupies the center place in our lives our circumstances adjust to reflect this. If the verse above is your experience then indeed "consider your ways" and put Jesus first in your life. When He has the place that is rightfully His in your heart then all your outward circumstances will correct themselves. This is certainly Haggai's message to the people of God in his day and given that the

Lord does not change *(Malachi 3:6)* it remains true today. Repair the House of the Lord in your locality!

The Kingdom of God speaks (1:7-11)

Again the people of God are challenged to "consider your ways!" They must go to the hills and get wood for the House of God because God wants to be glorified in His House through them. We are thus reminded that we serve together in a community which is called the Church of the living God. Ours is a corporate existence as the body of Christ and it is only as we share together, pray together, learn together and serve together that the fullness of Christ's life manifests amongst us. We are individually not the body, just parts of it and as we function together the body materializes and testifies to Jesus. This is the clear and unmistakable teaching of the New Testament; though many flout it and think that they can ignore the House of God.

> **"But now indeed there are many members, yet one body."**   **1 Corinthians 12:20**

> **"And let us consider one another in order to stir up love and good works, not forsaking the assembling of ourselves together, as is the habit of some, but exhorting one another, and so much the more as you see the Day approaching."**   **Hebrews 10:24-25**

The God of heaven is not content to allow this state of affairs to go unchallenged and so again He speaks to His people and asks them to consider that:

1. They never have enough money no matter how hard they may work,

2. They never get enough rain to nourish their crops,

3. They never get a good crop…..and,

4. They endure a drought that undermines the work of their hands.

Is God speaking to you? His Kingdom and the concerns of His House must be the major priority of your life and, if they are not, you are in trouble just as the people of Haggai's time were. Let us consider our ways.

The Kingdom of God delights in obedience (1:12-15; 2:1-5)

When we obey God we begin to live in what I call 'the super-normal." That is, God by Jesus Christ begins to take ordinary day things around us and He turns them into a unique blessing for us. Jesus did this when He used ordinary water to make wine and when He took a few fishes and a few loaves of bread and multiplied them. We can all live in the super-normal if we determine to get right with God and serve Him in complete obedience. You may say, "No one can serve Him in complete obedience?" Yes we can because this is a matter of desire and not one of performance. Here we are told that the moment the people obeyed God He responded to them by saying; "I am with you" (1:13). There can be no greater joy in life than to know that God is truly with you and not merely with you but stirring up the hearts of those around you who are also willing to serve Him obediently. This means firstly giving attention to His House. The lesson is clear: when we obey God He begins to work with us and this is truly encouraging.

Moreover and secondly, we are told in the beginning of the second chapter that, as a consequence of their obedience, God will give His House unparalleled glory but they are to be strong and work hard knowing that His Spirit is with them *(2:5)*. This also constitutes a wonderful promise for every local church today. Truly obedience is the key to the kingdom of God and of course Jesus underlined this time and time again in His teaching and many parables. Paul did the same when he wrote:

> **"What then? Shall we sin because we are not under law but under grace? Certainly not! Do you not know that to whom you present yourselves slaves to obey, you are that one's slaves whom you obey, whether of sin leading to death, or of obedience leading to righteousness? But God be thanked that though you were slaves of sin, yet you obeyed from the heart that form of doctrine to which you were delivered."**   **Romans 6:15-17**

Please take note that Paul put his finger on the heart of the matter when he writes, *"...yet you obeyed from the heart..."* This is the crucial issue facing the people of God then and now. This is further proved by the fact that the writer of the book of Hebrews, when encouraging the Jewish followers of Jesus not to give up but rather to live in continuing obedience to God, quotes from

Haggai. God will shake all things in heaven and on earth and so we must live in real union with Him and in obedience to Him because at the end of the day only those things built firmly on the kingdom of God will endure forever.

> **"See that you do not refuse Him who speaks. For if they did not escape who refused him who spoke on earth, much more shall we not escape if we turn away from Him who speaks from heaven, whose voice then shook the earth; but now He has promised, saying, 'Yet once more I shake not only the earth, but also heaven.' Now this, "Yet once more," indicates the removal of those things that are being shaken,as of things that are made, that the things that cannot be shaken may remain. Therefore, since we are receiving a kingdom which cannot be shaken, let us have grace, by which We may serve God acceptably with reverence and godly fear. For our God is a consuming fire."**
>
> **Hebrews 12:25-29**

The Kingdom of God is, and will be, the only reality (2:6-9)

Having shaken the people of God the Lord now turns to the nations and warns them that He is about to shake them as well. This shaking carries with it the idea that they will be judged and humbled and then they will ascend to Zion to a restored Temple to worship Him. The resting place of God in His glorious Temple will make this place of pilgrimage the "Desire of all nations" and, since the God of Israel owns all the gold and silver in the world, He will beautify His House in a way that is incredible. This restored Temple will be filled with God's majesty and His peace will reign over all the earth. "In this place I will give peace", says God, proving that peace is only something that the earth can have when it finally acknowledges Him and worships Him. We are still far away from this reality but it will come and of this we can all be sure.

The promises here are messianic and therefore remain ahead of us thus making this Mini Prophet so important as he reinforces the idea that God by Jesus Christ will triumph over the world and in the end Israel will find its way back to the glory of God. The Temple here referred to is a millennial temple from which the Messiah King will reign over the earth for a thousand years. Isaiah also wrote of this coming "day" and he tells us that peace will rein over the earth from Jerusalem and in particular from the *"House of the Lord"; consequently the nations "will learn war no more."*

> **"Now it shall come to pass in the latter days that the mountain of the Lord's house shall be established on the top of the mountains, and shall be exalted above the hills; and all nations shall flow to it. Many people shall come and say, 'Come, and let us go up to the mountain of the Lord, to the house of the God of Jacob; He will teach us His ways and we shall walk in His paths.' For out of Zion shall go forth the law and the word of the Lord from Jerusalem. He shall judge between the nations, and rebuke many people; they shall beat their spears into plowshares, and their spears into pruning hooks; nation shall not lift up sword against nation, neither shall they learn war anymore."**
>
> **Isaiah 2:2-4**

Also, it is worth noting that God warns a second time in this chapter that He intends to "shake heaven and earth" and He will "overthrow the throne of kingdoms" meaning quite plainly that He will break the power of the "… Gentile Kingdoms" *(2:22)*. His kingdom will thus triumph and so now we must serve it and recognize that in so doing we are building our lives on the only safe foundation that will not pass away. Abraham began his pilgrimage by looking for this "city" that "has foundations….whose architect and builder is God" *(Hebrews 11:9-10)*. We must do the same.

The Kingdom of God requires holy vigilance (2:10-19)

The presence, power and blessing of God are conditional upon His people's purity of life and practice. Nothing has changed and we should remember this. Here the priests are responsible for calling the people of God to holy living and God reminds them of this by referring, if you will, to the manual of ritual observance. All of this comes from the five books of Moses. There were thus rules relating to what was ritually unclean and clean. The word to Haggai is that the people are unclean just as these rules dictate. That is, they were not walking in holiness and consequently they did not experience the blessing of the super-normal in their lives. However, since the day they determined to obey God and make His House their priority things have changed in that God has blessed them. Again, the prophet underlines the crucial place that obedience should hold in our lives. We should thus be watchful and vigilant in this regard and particularly so the Shepherds of the Flock. Paul knew this as well and thus said to the leaders of his day:

> **"Therefore take heed to yourselves and to all the flock, among which the Holy Spirit has made you overseers, to shepherd the church of God which He purchased with His own blood."** Acts 20:28

The Kingdom of God's King (2:23)

This fascinating little book concludes with a promise to Zerubbabel, the Governor, that is unique and a picture of the Messiah. God will make him "like a signet ring; for I have chosen you." A signet ring is that which bears the title and emblem of the family and can be used, in certain cases, to emblazon these things upon special, important and regal documents. The holder of such a ring is the rightful heir of the family. Here Zerubbabel is promised God's signet ring! In reality it constitutes a promise of the coming of Messiah. That is, from his lineage Messiah Jesus would come as the unique and only one- of-a-kind Son of God. This truly happened because Luke, the Gospel writer, records that Zerubbabel was indeed a part of Messiah's lineage. (*Luke 3:27*)

All of this reminds us that our acts of obedience to the will of God will secure unique blessings for the generations that come from us. We can truly secure the future by caring for God's House today. Paul called this reaping what you sow and thus the awesome truth is that our futures are nothing less than what we are doing in the present.

> **"Do not be deceived, God is not mocked; for whatever a man sows, that he will also reap."** Galatians 6:7

DEVOTION

In Dangerous Times a Serious and Powerful Mission.

"Who is wise? Let him understand these things. Who is prudent? Let them know them. For the ways of the Lord are right; the righteous walk in them, but transgressors stumble in them." **Hosea 14:9**

The Mini Prophet Haggai calls attention to the fact that the House of God is in disrepair. It needs to be completed and made ready for the purposes of God so that once again the glory of God can inhabit it and fill the people of God with joy. Jesus said that His House should be chiefly a "House of Prayer for all nations" and thus He removed everything from it that contradicted this high holy calling. Today the Church of Jesus needs to be rebuilt and finished meaning that we should be loyal to it, put its welfare before our own and make it a "House of Prayer." If we do this truly, as Haggai points out, "the latter glory of this House will be greater than that of the first." The question is, will we rise to this challenge?-

One of the most troubling trends in the Church today is the neglect and devaluing of the power of prayer. This is yet another indication of a church in the world that is losing its commitment to biblical teaching that is so foundational to all that we are. It was Paul who said, "In everything by prayer let your requests be made known to God and..." (*Philippians 4: 6*). Prayer is the very backbone of our churches and nations. A prayerless church or nation is in serious trouble but, on the other hand, a church and nation at prayer is in a very safe and powerful place. It was Mary, the Queen of the Scots, who stated that what she feared most on earth was the prayers of the great reformer and preacher John Knox. She was right! He governed from his prayer closet and changed the course of history *(Psalm 149: 5-9)*. History proves time and time again that what happens on earth can be ordered by men and women of prayer *(Daniel 10:10-12)*. After all, in His greatest hour of need and purpose, Jesus retreated to the Garden of Gethsemane to pray. This last prayer vigil before His unique passion changed the world forever *(Luke 22: 39-46)*.

We could go on and on but the point is made and it is this: God answers prayer! It is equally true that great nations, like the USA and the United Kingdom, are at a "never seen before" crossroad in a very dangerous time in history. Dangers within and dangers without threaten the very fabric of our nations. From within we are witnessing an all out assault on the great Christian values that made these nations great. Political figures, with great ability and skill, but nevertheless with no biblical foundations, are pressing more and more for a political correct regime that essentially dismantles and sidelines the voice of Jesus in the nation. This in the end creates man in his own image, which in turn leads to the devaluing of life and the sanctioning of behavior that is ungodly and perverted. Once this step has been taken it is easy to abort babies and treat the precious gift of life as garbage to be thrown away. Euthanasia will follow and other evils and so the plunge away from God will take place; all in the name of love and of human rights and dignity. Those who sound the alarm are already being vilified and laughed at but the displeasure of God will result in His judgment if these evils are not corrected by repentance and prayer. This is the testimony of history.

From without rogue totalitarian regimes, like Iran and North Korea, are building weapons of mass destruction and in the process are unashamedly declaring their willingness to use them on Israel, Europe and the USA. The "Great Satan", the United States of America, must be overthrown as it is the home of the "infidel crusader." Its ally, the "Little Satan", Israel, must equally be destroyed and Russia is again flexing its muscles by challenging the West and America with its new policy of aggression in its sphere of influence. Throughout the Middle East we are witnessing a new and horrifying barbarism as militant Muslims march through the region beheading and killing all who do not agree with them. The carnage is mind-boggling but the focus of the world is upon Israel with the hope of turning its capital over to a Hamas led terrorist regime. This is the world that our nations face today. What do our nations need? The answer is prayer and lots of it! The Church should be deeply concerned about its lukewarm spiritual life and the future of our nations and its appropriate response should be a call to prayer as never before; but one never hears it.

Indeed darkness is closing in at every level of society and still the Church refuses to pick up its "weapons for the right hand and left", by which it can and should bring down mighty strongholds of darkness and sin (*2 Corinthians 10:1-6*). Waiting on God is hard work but if we do not get to this most holy work we will see a tidal wave of evil overtake us. The Prophet Joel gave just such an urgent call to prayer in his day. The truth is, the people were too otherwise occupied, ignored him, and were eventually overtaken by a huge national catastrophe. His words ring with urgency and concern

> **"Gird yourselves and lament you priests; wail, you who minister at the altar; come lie all night in sackcloth, you who minister to my God..." Consecrate a fast, call a sacred assembly; gather the elders and all the inhabitants of the land into the house of the Lord your God, and cry out to the Lord."**
> **Joel 1:13-14**

The questions we have to ask are, "when will we take upon ourselves the most holy and urgent work of prayer and when will our churches turn every meeting into a prayer meeting?" I fear that the answer will be, "Never!"

OBADIAH

**"But on Mount Zion there shall be
deliverance and there shall be
holiness; the house of Jacob shall
possess their possessions."**
Obadiah 17

Obadiah is an obscure post exilic Prophet with an explosive message that is
recorded in just one chapter. Essentially he sets out the struggle that began
in Rebekah's womb between two brothers, Jacob and Esau. This struggle
persisted through their lifetime and beyond and indeed Jacob, the cheat or
supplanter, contributed to it by deceiving his father and thereby stealing
Esau's birth- right *(Genesis 27:1-35)*. The reality, however, was that Esau had
sold his birth-right for a pot of stew and thus before God had forfeited it
(Genesis 25:29-34). Nevertheless, Jacob should have trusted God to get it and
should not have manipulated things by his carnal scheming. We can learn
from this in that we very often are too quick to "organize things" rather
than cultivating patience and waiting upon God to act. Like Abraham, who
fell into the same trap, we can "birth an Ishmael" and this in turn can be a
source of trouble for generations to come.

Esau represented something very sinister and evil and consequently God
loved Jacob but hated Esau *(Malachi 1:2-3)*. Here in this very short book Esau's
family is established east of Jerusalem in an impregnable mountain fortress
and they become known as Edom. The Edomites became implacable enemies
of Israel and sought every means possible to destroy them. However, there
is something more sinister about Edom than just a people group that hated

God and His people. This little book invites us to see this reality and to be warned by it. We therefore must now turn our attention to the following:

The call to spiritual conflict (1:1)

> **"Thus says the Lord concerning Edom (We have heard a report from the Lord, and a messenger has been sent among the nations, saying "Arise, and let us rise up against her for battle"): Behold I will make you small among the nations;"**

A "Messenger" in the Bible is an Angelic Watcher who goes forth to do the bidding of the Lord *(Daniel 4:23)*. Here the Messenger is calling for the destruction of Edom. Edom, at the very least is a terrifying and evil entity that threatens the well being of the nations and not just Israel. At the very least then this is a call to spiritual conflict that has to do with resisting evil. In his Ephesian letter Paul reminds us that we are indeed in a battle against something bigger than ourselves and that lurks behind and controls the world around us. He therefore writes that we do not "battle against flesh and blood but against principalities, against powers, against the rulers of the darkness of this age, against spiritual hosts of wickedness in the heavenly places" *(Ephesians 6:12)*. The moment you become a Christ follower this conflict begins and it is a deadly one. Indeed anything that finds its purpose in the will of God will encounter Edom! This is why Israel has always been in the "gun-sights" of Edom and still is.

The call to identify Edom (1:2-9)

As we have already noted, it is clear that Edom in this book is more than just a regional entity that opposed the people of God way back in time. The truth is Edom is the personification of the Devil or Lucifer. This is an entity that has attempted to ascend to the stars and is filled with pride and arrogance.

> **"The pride of your heart has deceived you, you who dwell in the clefts of the rock, whose habitation is high; you who say in your heart, "Who will bring me down to the ground?" Though you ascend as high as an eagle, and though you set your nest among the stars, from**

there I will bring you down," says the Lord."
Obadiah 1:3-4

We have the same principle in the books of Isaiah and Ezekiel where a regional entity is clearly a picture of the Devil's fall due to his pride and arrogance. So, in Ezekiel twenty–eight and verses twelve to seventeen the King of Tyre, a real earthly King, is personified as the Devil and the same is true of the King of Babylon in Isaiah fourteen verses twelve to fifteen.

> **"Son of man, take up a lamentation for the King of Tyre, and say to him, 'Thus says the Lord God: "You were the seal of perfection, full of wisdom and perfect in beauty. You were in Eden the garden of God; every precious stone was your covering: the sardius, topaz, and diamond, beryl, onyx and jasper, sapphire, turquoise, and emerald with gold. The workmanship of your timbrels and pipes was prepared for you on the day you were created. You were the anointed cherub who covers; I established you; you were on the holy mountain of God; you walked back and forth in the midst of fiery stones. You were perfect in your ways from the day you were created, till iniquity was found in you. By the abundance of your trading you became filled with violence within, and you sinned; therefore I cast you as a profane thing out of the mountain of God; and I destroyed you, O covering cherub, from the midst of the fiery stones. Your heart was lifted up because of your beauty; you corrupted your wisdom for the sake of your splendor; I cast you to the ground before kings, that they might gaze at you."** Ezekiel 28:12-17

> **"How you have fallen from heaven, O Lucifer, son of the morning! How you are cut down to the ground, you who weakened the nations! For you said in your heart; I will ascend into heaven, I will exalt my throne above the stars of God; I will also sit on the mount of the congregation on the farthest sides of the north; I will ascend above the heights of the clouds, I will be like the Most High. Yet you shall be brought down to Sheol, the to the lowest depths of the pit."** Isaiah 14:12-15

Edom is the same; he dominates the world system and subjugates the nations and hates Israel. God will bring him down as well.

All this reminds us of the very real presence of evil in the world and not just because the human race rebelled against God and thereby embraced it. No, there is a sinister being in the world that is incredibly powerful and determined to frustrate God's purpose and bring to destruction every man, woman and child. We, by our own strength cannot defeat him, but, by the blood of Christ we can. But even here we may have to forfeit our very lives in doing so and many have. John writes:

> **"And they overcame him by the blood of the Lamb and by the word of their testimony, and they did not love their lives to the death."** **Revelation 12:11**

Also, we learn in all of this that the Devil is very near; Esau was Jacob's brother, Judas was one of the twelve *(Luke 6:16)* and Jesus said that he was a "devil" and even Peter gave voice to the Devil's desire when he tried to dissuade Jesus from going to the cross *(John 6:70, Matthew 16:23)*. Whenever the word of God is truly preached the Devil is at hand to rob its impact from those who hear it *(Luke 8:12)* and indeed he controls and dominates the world *(1 John 5:19)*. Moreover, anyone who does not know Christ is dominated and bound by him *(Ephesians 2:1-2)* and those who do know Christ are constantly under threat of demonic attack *(1Peter 5:8-9)*. This is no game and we must keep our lives pure, stay out of the world system *(Revelation 18:4)* and resist Edom. Jesus gives us the victory.

The call to understand Edom's strategy (1:10-16)

> **"For violence against your brother Jacob, shame shall cover you, and you shall be cut off forever."**
>
> **Obadiah 1:10**

Edom stood by and rejoiced when Israel was besieged, conquered and taken into captivity by the Babylonians. Indeed from the very beginning Edom did everything in its power to frustrate the plan of God flowing through Israel to the world. In fact Edom engaged the nations with one goal in mind and that was to defeat and destroy Israel. Nothing has changed! Edom has continued to rampage through history with the never ending desire to remove every last Jew from the earth. We saw this in the persecutions of history; (sadly motivated mostly by those who claimed to be Christ followers) in the Holocaust and in the present day Islamic strategy to liquidate the restored state of Israel. Edom is also behind the rise of anti-Semitism in the world and he is determined to pursue this aged old hatred of Zion. The conflict of the ages is now truly upon us but God will bring him down and remove him from the face of the earth forever.

This "Day" of recompense to Edom, for all that it has done to Israel and the nations, will arrive when the Day of the Lord befalls the world (*1:15-16*). This is yet ahead of us but actually just around the corner! The fact that the Edomites, as a people group, vanished centuries ago proves that Edom is a sinister and wicked entity that finds its ultimate expression and continuing existence in the Devil and his fallen hordes. Edom is still with us today but his final and irretrievable fall is coming. God by Jesus Christ will see to it. It is also interesting to note from these verses that the nations that willingly allied themselves with Edom, in the desire to destroy Israel, will suffer a terrifying judgment and will fall with her.

The call to understand God's strategy (1:17-21)

> **"But on Mount Zion there shall be deliverance, and there shall be holiness; the house of Jacob shall possess their possessions."** Obadiah 1:17

Obadiah's short but wonderful and very powerful oracle ends with a promise of God's deliverance of Israel, and indeed the world, from Edom's tyranny. This is good news indeed and it reminds us that God has not abandoned our world to the forces of wickedness and evil; that is, to the evil of Edom. Righteousness, peace and joy are soon coming to the entire world but they do fill the hearts of those who love Jesus now (*Romans 14:17*). So then Obadiah tells us the following:

1. The holy people of Israel will be delivered. This is an absolute certainty and therefore it is a confidence and prayer booster as we look at the Middle East region today that appears to be so dark and beyond remedy. God will do it!

2. The holy people of Israel will, by virtue of their struggle against Edom and the nations allied with him, become a holy people indeed. God always expected them to be a holy nation and to

exemplify the light that they have received and radiated to the nations (Exodus 19:5-6).

3. The holy people of Israel will inherit the land of Canaan here called "their possessions." God decided four thousand years ago that Israel would inherit Canaan as an everlasting possession *(Genesis 17:7-8)*. He has not changed His mind and He will in the end humble the nations and even the Church who have relentlessly questioned this inheritance. We should learn from this not to gain say God.

4. A holy people will be given renewed power and ability to overcome their enemies. We are told, "the house of Jacob shall be a fire, and the house of Joseph a flame; but the house of Esau shall be stubble" *(v18)*. Zechariah, the restoration Prophet, speaking of these same days, says that Israel will be emboldened by God to overcome all of her enemies in the end time *(Zechariah 12:5-9)*. We saw just a glimpse of this in the now famous Six Day War of June 1967 when Israel literally ran over her enemies who were greater in strength and fire power but they nevertheless became stubble. More of this is to come.

5. A holy people will be comforted by a great Aliyah that will augment her numbers and bring most of her dispersed children home. This process has already begun which serves as another reminder that we are living in extraordinary days. And finally,

6. A holy family of Deliverers or Christ followers will come to Mt. Zion and "judge the mountains of Esau." Consequently, the "kingdom shall be the Lord's." Here is a promise of Jesus' coming to Jerusalem with all His saints to cast out Edom and rule the nations. Oh what a blessed day that will be and it is promised throughout scripture. For instance Jesus Himself said:

"And he who overcomes, and keeps My works until the end, to him I will give power over the nations-He shall rule them with a rod of iron; they shall be dashed to pieces like the potter's vessels-as I also received from My Father." **Revelation 2:26-27**

When Jesus comes with all His saints to rule the world in righteousness the Devil will be bound and the world, once under the dominion of Edom, will be covered with the knowledge and glory of the Lord "as the waters cover the sea" *(Isaiah 11:9)* Israel's role in history will be vindicated and the nations will learn war no more. Obadiah leaves us with a marvelous vision of hope!

DEVOTION

The Armor of God

"Finally, my brethren, be strong in the Lord and in the power of His might. Put on the whole armor of God, that you may be able to stand against the wiles of the devil. For we do not wrestle against flesh and blood, but against principalities, against powers, against the rulers of the darkness of this age, against spiritual hosts of wickedness in the heavenly places. Therefore take up the whole armor of God, that you may be able to withstand in the evil day, and having done all, to stand.

Stand therefore, having girded your waist with truth, having put on the breastplate of righteousness, and having shod your feet with the preparation of the gospel of peace; above all, taking the shield of faith with which you will be able to quench all the fiery darts of the wicked one. And take the helmet of salvation, and the sword of the Spirit, which is the word of God; praying always with all prayer and supplication in the Spirit, being watchful to this end with all perseverance and supplication for all the saints—and for me, that utterance may be given to me, that I may open my mouth boldly to make known the mystery of the gospel, for which I am an ambassador in chains; that in it I may speak boldly, as I ought to speak."

Ephesians 6:10-20

The Mini Prophet Obadiah teaches us that we have an enemy that is unseen, real and determined to destroy us just as he is determined to destroy Israel. Edom, a clear picture of a demonic reality, is always lurking in the background seeking "whom he may devour" (*1 Peter 5:8-9*). This is a real battle that can only be fought with real spiritual weapons and we must make sure that we are well equipped to embrace it and be victorious in it.

Here in this famous passage of the book of Ephesians we have Paul's exhortation to be ready for battle by adorning the armor of God. In this regard he employs an illustration that was very familiar to him in that wherever he went in the Middle East, Asia and beyond the Roman soldier was everywhere observable. He was a formidable force to be reckoned with as he, together with his legions, had conquered the then known world. For Paul then he was an excellent example of what a Christian should be in a more dangerous and formidable battle that rages in the unseen spiritual world.

Key words

Paul's opening statement to this important passage contains some key words that we should take note of. Firstly that we should be "strong in the Lord;" God wants His people, saved by the blood of Jesus, to be strong. It is in the Lord that we can only become strong but we have to pursue God's strength and appropriate it. Weak Christians are those that have failed to fully embrace the grace of God that is flowing toward them in Christ Jesus. There are far too many of these around. God our Father wants us to be clothed with His power and might.

Secondly, we are called upon to embrace the "whole armor of God" and not just one part of it. This armor of God is made up of key Christian truths that we have to own if we are ever going to be victorious and useful to Jesus. If one piece is missing we will become vulnerable to an enemy that will fully exploit this "gap" and cause us untold trouble.

Thirdly, we are up against the Devil; an unseen but very real entity that is very powerful and has stratagems in place to de-rail our spiritual well being. This is no idle threat and it must be remembered that Paul is writing to Christians. They are the target of the Devil's wiles and if they do not take up the whole armor of God they will make themselves weak and vulnerable to demonic attack and many have. Truly, we are up against vast and very powerful wicked principalities in heavenly places.

Key components

The armor of God is really vital truths that have to get from our minds into our hearts so that they become a real part of us. According to Paul an "evil day" comes to all of us and woe to us if we are not properly clad in the armor of God. A Roman soldier going into battle had to give careful attention to the condition of his armor, both offensive and defensive, and so he had to ensure that it was tight fitting and properly secured to his body; if not he would be in serious trouble when the battle was engaged. For Paul the Christian soldier has to give attention to:

1. **The belt of truth (V14a)**This truth is the truth of God's Word in its entirety. The "belt" that the Roman soldier secured around his waist was the most important piece of his armor as it, when properly employed, held all the other pieces of his armor in place. Every Christian should live in the Word of God day and night. Jesus said that God's Word was truth (John 17:17) and that it should be the daily food that feeds our souls (Matthew 4:4). If we have no idea of the parameters of God's dealing with us we shall never be able to stand and fight. The sin of neglecting the Bible is rife in the Church and this is precisely why the wider Church is so weak and ineffective in the world. Consequently the powers of darkness have very little to do; the Church has already been immobilized.

2. **The breastplate of righteousness** *(V14b)* The Christian must know in his heart that Jesus' death on the cross has fully satisfied the demands of God's character on his behalf and thus he or she has forever been delivered from the consequences of their sins, past, present and future, and therefore God declares that they are perfect in Christ before Him and righteous *(2 Corinthians 5:21)*. He sees nothing in us that attracts His displeasure *(Romans 5:1)*. The Devil will always attempt to undermine this concept of right standing with God in our lives and so we have to resist thoughts of any type that undermine this blessed position that is ours in Christ. Naturally, you have to couple this with a mind that also desires for and seeks the righteousness of Christ. If a sincere Christian believes that God is displeased with him then the powers of darkness will quickly neutralize him. You heart must be covered with a breastplate that assures you of your righteous position in Christ.

3. **The feet shod with the Gospel** *(V15)* The powerful weapon that God has given us is the Gospel message. We walk with our feet and so wherever we go we should tell people the Good News of Jesus. A soldier cannot advance in any direction that pleases him; if he does he will be wounded or killed. No, he has a mission that drives him ever forward with his fellow warriors and in this way victory is secured. The Gospel is a message that tells the world of the Devil's utter and complete defeat and so, indeed, it is the single thing that he will resist most. You must stand up firm in your resolve to share the Gospel. This is what you are fighting for. A soldier that loses his shoes will lose his grip, falter and fail and so it is with Christians.

4. **The shield of faith** *(V16)* Faith believes what God says even if this "saying of God" contradicts what we see, feel and smell *(Hebrews 11:1)*. This is why faith comes by hearing the word of God *(Romans 10:17)*; we need to know what God says! The Bible says that we have all received a measure of faith that we have to grow and strengthen like a muscle *(Romans 12:3)*. God will call us into faith adventures commensurate with our growth and thereby teach us to trust Him. This is a journey that we must all welcome and embrace. It is an exciting one as the more we overcome by faith so the more Jesus will gives us bigger faith hurdles to mount or projects to undertake for Him. The shield gave the Roman soldier protection when the enemy launched fiery arrows against him. In like manner if you know God's word a fiery arrow launched by the powers of darkness will not penetrate you because you know the truth.

5. **The helmet of salvation** *(V17a)* The helmet gave protection to the head and so for Paul the most dangerous "battle ground" we face is that of the mind. What gets hold of you mind will get hold of your emotions and what gets hold of your emotions will dictate and control your actions. Remember; garbage in means garbage out! It all starts in the mind. The Bible exhorts Christians, time and time again, to guard and protect their minds *(1 Peter 1:13; Philippians 4:8-9; Romans 12:1-2; Ephesians 4:21-24)*. Your mind is a veritable gateway to your soul and what gets into it is important; very important. No tool has been used more to subvert the minds of people than television and its internet counterparts. Whole generations are being destroyed by these appliances. Inherently, there is nothing wrong with them but they have to be regulated or con-

trolled otherwise we end up feeding our minds on filth which in turn grieves the Holy Spirit. The result; a Christian that is useless to God.

6. **The sword of the Spirit** *(V17b)* Christians must not simply know the Word of God they must be able to use it as a weapon. The Bible is not merely a defensive instrument, by which we protect our spiritual lives, but it is also an offensive weapon whereby we advance Christ's Kingdom in the world. We are moving forward against our enemy and we do so effectively with the Word of God in our hands. Jesus employed the Word of God in this manner during His encounter with the Devil on the Mount of Temptation recorded in the fourth chapter of Matthew. It is to be noted that Paul does not give us armor that covers our backs! The reason is simple; we are always victorious because of what Jesus has done and so we always take spiritual ground for Him by going forward. We can only do this if we have the sword of God's Word in our hands. We must use it confidently and in every which way possible because it is two edged.

7. **Praying always** *(V18)* Soldiers in the Roman army, as in all armies, had war-cries and songs whereby they expressed their belief in the regime and system that they represented. These were verbalized always and everywhere and, naturally speaking, gave them confidence and courage. As Christians we have prayer as our source of strength and power and by which we depend on God's presence to give us victory. We should pray always and for everything, according to Paul *(Philippians 4:6; 1 Thessalonians 5:17)*. Prayer is to be the spiritual breath that we breathe and it should encompass all that we do in life. The Church today is weak because it has abandoned prayer in favor of a slick methodology. We do this to our peril because by so doing we disconnect ourselves from our source of power and the Devil knows it well! We must learn to build strong prayer lives.

Finally, Paul reminds his readers that he represents everything that he has been writing about in terms of the armor of God and so he requests prayer since he is a preacher of the Gospel, an Ambassador for Christ and a prisoner for Jesus. *(6:19-20)* Nevertheless, he is undeterred and desires only that he should preach more powerfully the message of Jesus. The message is clear; Paul led by example.

———•———

JOEL

**"And it shall come to pass that
whoever calls on the name of the
Lord shall be saved."**

Joel 2:32

Joel, meaning Yahweh is God, is a pre-exilic Prophet who gives meaning and interpretation to a natural disaster in the form of what I call a "locust attack" that befell Israel in his day. This plague of locusts brought the nation to the brink of disaster and Joel warned that the real issue is the nation's ungodliness and rebellion against God. Unless urgently rectified, by prayer, fasting and fruits of repentance, the awful Day of the Lord will overtake them and "blow" them away. Nations today that ignore the "real voice and meaning" of natural disasters should take a leaf out of Joel's oracle.

Joel's prophecy actually goes further than simply addressing Israel in that it focuses on the nations and in particular on their relentless attempts to divide the land of Israel and thereby disinvest Israel of it. They are messing with God and will pay a terrible price for it because He, consequently, is calling for war! So then, Joel's prophecy, though dire, carries within it a promise of the outpouring of the Holy Spirit that will not only refresh Israel but indeed "all flesh." Like the other Mini Prophets, he sees beyond the day at hand and gives us a vision of the future that is both good and bad depending on where you stand with the God of the Bible.

Devastation (1:1-12)

"What the chewing locust left, the swarming locust has eaten; what the swarming locust left, the crawling locust has eaten; and what the crawling locust left, the consuming locust has eaten."   **Joel 1:4**

Joel draws attention to the fact that the plague of locusts was unique in Israel's history and that this in itself should make the leaders, people and children wake up to the fact that God is speaking to them about their sinful way of living in that they were given to drunkenness and rebellion against God. They should be ashamed of their conduct since the arrival of a devastating plague of locusts was God's response to their wickedness. However, if there is no repentance in Zion, there will be a more devastating plague coming in the form of the Babylonian army which is on the march toward Jerusalem *(V6-10)*. The result will be a devastation of the land and its economy and so the agricultural support system and even the daily priestly rituals in the Temple will cease. When the House of God in a nation dies then the nation surely plunges into darkness and history is littered with examples of this. Nevertheless, the arrogance of the human heart is such that it will not hear God speaking in natural catastrophes, conflicts and upheavals; preferring rather to blame these on everything else but the response of God to their wickedness. Hurricane Katrina that struck New Orleans and beyond is a clear example of this in that this catastrophe called for repentance but none was forthcoming. The book of Revelation confirms this as, even though God is reaching out to the world in judgment; in the form of a new plague of locusts *(Revelation 9:3, 6-8)*, it refuses to repent *(Revelation 16:9)*. In recent years natural disasters and conflicts have raged through our world but it will not listen to the real voice behind them all and so the nations, like Israel of old, are marching toward judgment and when it arrives it will be complete just like the devastation that the chewing, swarming and crawling locusts brought to Israel of old. The God we serve is not given to change. Joel's oracle constitutes a serious warning to the nations today and a challenge to the Church in the nations to be a true prophetic voice. Though our nations are filled with churches, of "all stripes and colors", the truth is, history will affirm that "the word of the Lord was rare in those days" *(1 Samuel 3:1)*. We too should be ashamed.

Consecration (1:13-14; 2:12-17)

> "Gird yourselves and lament, you priests; wail, you who minister before the altar; come, lie all night in sackcloth, you who minister to my God; for the grain offering and the drink offering are withheld from the house of your God. Consecrate a fast, call a sacred assembly; gather the elders and all the inhabitants of the land into the house of the Lord your God, and cry out to the Lord."
>
> Joel 1:13-14

> "Now, therefore, "says the Lord, turn to Me with all your heart, with fasting, with weeping, and with mourning." So rend your heart, and not your garments return to the Lord your God, for He is gracious and merciful, slow to anger and of great kindness; and He relents from doing harm."
>
> Joel 2:12-13

> "Blow the trumpet in Zion, consecrate a fast, call a sacred assembly; gather the people, sanctify the congregation, assemble the elders, gather the children and nursing babes; let the bridegroom go out from his chamber and the bride from her dressing room. Let the priests, who minister to the Lord, weep between the porch and the altar; let them say, "Spare Your people O Lord, and do not give Your heritage to reproach, that the nations should rule over them..."
>
> Joel 2:15-17

Here we have a record of what should be the urgent spiritual business of the day. The blowing of the trumpet is an alarm that warns of impending danger. The people of Zion are called to wake up spiritually to the very real danger that is facing them and about to overwhelm them. Everyone, even the bride and bridegroom, are to run to the place of repentance, fasting and prayer. The God they serve will respond quickly to their cry because He is gracious, kind and full of mercy and desires to bless them. What a wonderful God we serve.

As it was then, so it is today; the people of God do not pray and they ignore the fact that Jesus said that His House "is to be a House of Prayer for all nations" *(Matthew 21:13)*. Today His House is a house of preaching, a house of teaching, a house of singing and even a house of entertainment but sadly, not a house of prayer. The weekly prayer meeting, if it exists, is very badly attended while the vast majority of Christians prefer to watch television at home. They lament the state of the world and the threat that this poses to their well being but they will not be part of the solution; even though they know that there is absolutely no alternative. The trumpet is being blown but no one obeys the meaning of its sound. We are just like the people of Israel who came out of Egypt in that we prefer the road of celebration to that of consecration! Joshua once told Moses that there was a noise of war in the camp of Israel. In his mind this meant that the people were gearing up to take on the Lord's battles. Moses responded thus:

> **"It is not the noise of the shout of victory, nor the noise of the cry of defeat, but the sound of singing I hear."**
> **Exodus 32:18**

This perceptive statement by Moses just about sums it all up; they were not in a place of victory or defeat but in a place of having a good time. Church is not about having a good time; no it is about war and this war is only won in the place of importunate prayer. That is, prayer that is corporate, continuous, involves everyone in the community and that leads to victory and not to defeat. The need today, as it was in Joel's time, is consecration and this means that we have to learn how to use our very real and powerful spiritual weapons.

> **"For though we walk in the flesh, we do not war according to the flesh. For the weapons of our warfare are not carnal but mighty in God for the pulling down strongholds."** **2 Corinthians 10:3-4**

Destruction (1:15-20; 2:1-11)

> **"Alas for the day! For the day of the Lord is at hand; it shall come as destruction from the Almighty."**
> **Joel 1:15**

This awesome and terrible day of the Lord is about to roll over Israel and the instrument of God's choice by which to bring it upon Zion is the Babylonian army. They will run on the city and they will run on the walls because they will be the great army of destruction carrying out the word and purpose of the Lord *(V8-11)*. Quite plainly the day of destruction is at hand and the people of God have not responded as God asked them to; with repentance fasting and prayer. History now affirms this and so in 586 BC the Babylonians destroyed Jerusalem, killed thousands of people and took the remnant of the people into exile. It was a terrifying day that came upon a people that could have avoided it. Jeremiah's Lamentation testifies to this as does Joel's oracle.

It is clear from these verses that we are looking at something far greater in judgment than that which befell Jerusalem some 2600 years ago now. All of scripture, including the New Testament scriptures, warns of a great Day of the Lord that will befall the world *(1 Thessalonians 5:1-3; Revelation 6:12-17)*. God is going to bring destruction to the nations because they too have chosen wickedness over righteousness and it's not as if they didn't know since the revelation of God's existence and His righteous claims over their lives are made plain to them by what they see in nature and by what is stamped upon their consciences. Paul confirms this when he writes:

> **"For the wrath of God is revealed from heaven against all ungodliness and unrighteousness of men, who suppress the truth in unrighteousness, because what may be known of God is manifest in them, for God has shown it to them. For since the creation of the world His invisible attributes are clearly seen, being understood by the things that are made, even His eternal power and Godhead, so that they are without excuse."** **Romans 1:18-20**

Once again it is worth noting that all the Mini Prophets speak of the great Day of the Lord. Indeed the Major and Minor Prophets do so at length. It is thus a recurring theme and yet it is hardly referred to in preaching today. Why would this be, especially when we see ungodliness and evil abounding everywhere? The reason is simple: It might upset people and indeed in most cases we want them to leave Church with good and positive feelings and not negative ones!

Rehabilitation *(2:18-27)*

> **"Then the Lord will be zealous for His land, and pity His people. The Lord will answer and say to His people, "Behold, I will send you grain and new wine and oil, and you will be satisfied by them; I will no longer make you a reproach among the nations." Joel 2:18-19**

> **"Be glad then, you children of Zion, and rejoice in the Lord your God; for He has given you the former rain faithfully, and He will cause the rain to come down for you-the former rain, and the latter rain in the first month."**

> **Joel 2:21-23**

> **"I will restore to you the years that the swarming locust has eaten."**

> **Joel 2:25**

We have here painted for us a very beautiful picture of God's love, kindness, mercy and care for His people Israel. He longs to rehabilitate them and fill them with joy. Such will be the nature of His blessings that they will overflow, fill them with satisfaction and restore to them the years that the locust has eaten. Their God will send them the annual rain fall all at once and so twice a year they will have the former and latter rains together. Thus will God deal with a people that honor and love Him. There is here a promise for the Church as well since we desperately need an out pouring of spiritual rain upon us. Moreover, it is a fact that many of God's children, who came to faith in Jesus in their latter or middle years, decry the fact that they have wasted so many years in ungodliness and sin. But here we are told that God, by Jesus Christ, can roll these wasted years into our future and make them a blessing. Nothing will be lost and all our years will be His. Only a great God of love and grace can do this.

Also, it is worth noting that when God rehabilitates His people Israel He refers to their land as His *(V18)*. This is the issue facing the nations and He will yet deal with them over it and it will not go well for them.

Saturation (2:28-32)

> "And it shall come to pass afterward that I will pour out My Spirit on all flesh; your sons and your daughters shall prophesy, your old men shall dream dreams, your young men shall see visions. And also on My menservants and on My maidservants I will pour out My Spirit in those days." Joel 2:28-29

Here Joel gives a prophetic vision that sees into the very heart of the finished work of Jesus on the cross. A work that not only purchased the salvation of the world by His death, burial and resurrection but which also purchased the gift and outpouring of the Holy Spirit upon those who embrace Him as Lord.

> "This Jesus God has raised up, of which we are all witnesses. Therefore being exalted to the right hand of God, and having received from the Father the promise of the Holy Spirit, He poured out this which you now see and hear."
>
> Acts 2:32-33

God will now pour out His Spirit upon "all flesh" and not just Israel. This outpouring of God's Spirit will bring God close to His people in a way never seen or experienced before and so they will be saturated with His love. By His Spirit His people will dream dreams from heaven, see visions of the purpose of God and prophesy in new languages. Men, women and children will rejoice in the goodness, love and blessing of God and all this will refresh Israel and the people of God everywhere before the great and terrible Day of the Lord arrives. Jesus called this the Baptism of the Holy Spirit and all God's children should claim it by faith (*Acts 1:4-5*).

> "For the promise is to you and to your children, and to all who are a far off, as many as the Lord our God will call." Acts 2:39

Of course this great prophetic word of Joel was fulfilled on the Day of Pentecost just fifty days after Jesus rose from the dead. It is beautifully recorded by Luke in the second chapter of his book called the Acts of the Apostles. Fire, in the form of tongues, came from heaven and completely overshadowed the waiting apostles. Once timid and scared they now rose with boldness and courage to declare God's word to their generation. They had a new power by which to impact their world *(Acts 2: 1-4) (Acts 2:14)*. Jesus had spoken of this day when He said:

> **"Behold, I send the Promise of My Father upon you; but tarry in the city of Jerusalem until you are endued with power from on high."** Luke 24:49

According to Joel this outpouring of God's Spirit will impact Israel again just before the arrival of the great Day of the Lord and so he tells us that, "in Mount Zion and in Jerusalem there shall be deliverance" *(Joel 2:32)*. The Prophet Zechariah also speaks of this day in a more comprehensive way in that he states that God will pour out upon Jerusalem the Spirit of supplication and grace and consequently their eyes will be opened to see the true messianic credentials of Jesus and so they "will mourn for Him as one mourns for an only son" *(Zechariah 12:10-11)*. It is worth noting that every passage in the Bible dealing with the consummation of the age presents the Jews back in the land of their forefathers but more particularly, back in Jerusalem. That is, old biblical Jerusalem or what we call the Old City today. This is by God's doing and blessing and it provokes a global hatred of the Jews and an attempt to disinvest them of the city. This day is upon us but the Prophet will now go on to remind us that God will indeed have the last word on this matter.

Indignation (3:1-16)

> **"For behold, in those days and at that time, when I bring back the captives of Judah and Jerusalem, I will also gather all nations, and bring them down to the Valley of Jehoshaphat; and I enter into judgment with them there on account of My people, My heritage Israel, whom they have scattered among the nations; they have also divided up My land."** Joel 3:1-2

> **"Proclaim this among the nations: Prepare for war"!** Joel 3:9

Israel's existence, calling and journey have been and are for the blessing of the nations *(Genesis 12:1-3)*. This blessing is salvation blessing that leads to eternal life and so in order to enable her to discharge this mandate God gave her land; that is, the land of Canaan as an everlasting possession *(Genesis 17:7-8)*. But He gave it to her as a "tenant" in that it is actually His, making Him the "landlord." The nations, far from recognizing the huge blessing that Israel is to them, have hated her and done everything possible to destroy her and disinvest her of her land. They have repeatedly "divided up My land." This incurs the indignation of God and those who do it are truly playing with fire.

In reality then the never ending attack against the Jews is an attack against God and therefore an attempt to remove Him from the world. The nations wish to break God's bonds and cords from them since they hate righteousness and love evil and are motivated by the powers of darkness *(Psalm 2:1-2)*. Anti-Semitism then is humankind's anger at and rejection of God and since the Jews are the visible reminder of God in the world this anger is directed against them. In short, to remove God from the world one would first have to remove the Jews from it since they represent, in their existence, His power and existence. David knew this truth well and wrote of it in Psalm 83. This not only confirms the nations to judgment but it deeply angers God and so He will mobilize the nations for war! They may say peace, peace but there will be no peace because God is calling for war. So, Joel writes:

> **"Let the nations be wakened, and come up to the Valley of Jehoshaphat; for there I will sit to judge all the surrounding nations. Put in the sickle, for the harvest is ripe. Come, go down; for the wine press is full, the vats overflow- for their wickedness is great."**
>
> **Joel 3:12-13**

Joel has seen beyond our time into the days now just before us. All this, he says, will take place at a time when God brings the captives of Zion home to His Land *(3:1)*. We have witnessed this in our time after two thousand years of Jewish dispersion. We are also witnessing an unprecedented global attempt to divide up the land that is God's and even to wrest Jerusalem from Jewish control. We must sound the alarm because days of terrifying judgment are ahead of us and who will be able to stand?

Restoration (3:14-21)

> **"So you shall know that I am the Lord your God, dwelling in Zion My holy mountain. Then Jerusalem**

> **shall be holy, and no aliens shall ever pass through her**
> **again."**   **Joel 3:17**

Joel's dramatic oracle ends with a picture of deliverance and restoration in Israel. The hordes of the nations will be gathered in the "valley of decision" and the Lord will roar from Zion against them. They will be utterly devastated and destroyed, as the sun and the moon grow dark, but Israel will be divinely sheltered and saved out of these great days of tribulation *(V14-16)*. This picture of the end time occurs time and time again in the Bible and even Jesus referred to it *(Matthew 24:29)*. It is definitely ahead of us, just around the corner as it were, and we would do well to be on God's side at this time. That is, if He sees fit to defend a restored nation of Israel against a global onslaught then it would be good for us to do the same now by praying for Israel, standing with Israel, fighting anti-Semitism and helping Israel.

Israel will emerge saved and intact after this final conflict of history. Her enemies will be vanquished, the blessing of God will rain down upon her and her land will yield an abundance of wine, milk and water. all pictures of prosperity and joy. God will be at rest in Jerusalem and the Jewish people will "abide forever" *(V19-21)*. Only the redeemed of the Lord will occupy God's holy hill and this happy throng of the redeemed will include peoples from all the nations who have been grafted into Israel and thus are no longer gentiles, but truly a part of the great commonwealth of Israel *(Ephesians 2:11-13)*. An alien will no longer trample underfoot Zion! Blessed be the God of Israel.

DEVOTION

The Fall of Western Civilization

"But what is the explanation of the enslavement of Europe by the German Nazi regime? It is but a few years ago since one united gesture by the peoples, great and small, who are now broken in the dust, would have warded off from mankind the fearful ordeal it has to undergo. But there was no unity. There was no vision. The nations were pulled down one by one while the others gaped and chattered. One by one, each in his turn, they let themselves be caught. One after another they were felled by brutal violence or poisoned from within by subtle intrigue."
Winston Churchill 1941

The Mini Prophet Joel writes of a day when the nations will be brought down into judgment because of their wickedness and their ungodly and dishonest dealings with Israel. They have allowed Anti-Semitism to thrive and grow, have divided the land of Israel and, abandoning truth, have sold the children of Israel into the hands of their enemies. They have also dishonored the God who made them great and so He will gather them for a terrifying day of wrath.

"Proclaim this among the nations: "Prepare for War"!
Joel 3:9

"Multitudes, multitudes in the valley of decision! For the day of the Lord is near in the valley of decision. The sun and moon will grow dark, and the stars will

> **diminish their brightness. The Lord will roar from Zion, and utter His voice from Jerusalem; the heavens and earth will shake; but the Lord will be a shelter for His people, and the strength of the children of Israel."**
> **Joel 3:14-16**

The moral clarity, by which the western world defeated Nazism some seventy years ago, is now a thing of the past. Since World War Two the Western democracies, led mainly by naïve liberals, have allowed millions of Muslims to "set up shop" in their countries driven by the belief that they will fully integrate into their adopted societies and become proudly British, European and Scandinavian. This wildly misguided experiment at multi-culturalism has totally failed in that just the opposite has happened; they instead set up Saudi Arabia, Yemen, Algeria, Qatar, Pakistan, Syria etc in their host countries. They thus became Muslim outposts with every intention of subverting the host culture and replacing it with their own. They have therefore steadily and progressively, as they have gained strength of numbers, demanded that the legal system be changed to accommodate Sharia Law and that the banking system include Islamic principles. This is called "stealth jihad."

Consequently, as time has gone by, in order to accommodate these demands the traditional culture and belief system of the majority has been progressively surrendered all in the name of being politically correct and sensitive to minority groups. A report on the 28th August 2014 stated that Muslim men had abused some 1400 British Muslim girls. In response a former Labor Party Member of Parliament, Denis Mac Shane said, "I think there was a culture of not wanting to rock the multicultural community boat, if I may put it like that." He further stated that, "he had been aware of the oppression of women within bits of the Muslim community in Britain but perhaps yes, as a true Guardian reader, and liberal lefty, I suppose I didn't want to raise that too hard." This then typifies the danger of seeing everything through a political correct lens; evil is allowed to thrive! It is also opens the door to harassment as a Muslim seeing a cross on a pendant at the work place, can now claim that he or she is offended by it and that the offending fellow worker should be sanctioned and indeed is! This is outrageous. In the United Kingdom therefore aspects of Sharia Law have been implemented as has Islamic Banking and there are Muslim community areas that are in effect "no go" areas for non Muslims. Many of these "Muslim enclaves" in Britain, France,

Holland, Norway, Belgium and Sweden are being radicalized by Imams who are giving verbal and material support to Islamic terror organizations in the Middle East and beyond. Consequently a new phenomenon is emerging in that "home grown" jihadists are now growing in number and are attacking their own countries and going abroad to join barbaric organizations like Hamas, Hezbollah, Al-Qaida, and Isis. Three issues unite them all in that they hate the West, Jews and Israel.

This Muslim cultural invasion of the West is gaining strength with every passing day so that now, emboldened by this growth; intimidation and death threats are the norm and are leveled at anyone who may dare to criticize them. All of this is happening in western countries where law, order and free speech are enshrined and highly prized as a civilized reality. Universities, where young people are prepared for this civilized behavior, have become hotbeds of radicalization and so, if one disagrees with their narrative, one will be assaulted, shouted down and never given a fair hearing; especially if you are Jewish or Israeli or espouse traditional Christian beliefs. Gert Wilders, a well known Dutch politician, who dared to make his voice heard on these matters and thereby defied the politically correct culture of his land, was consequently subjected to death threats and was hauled up before the Dutch courts on groundless charges; all of which denied his rights as a Dutch citizen. He won in the end but at a great price. He found out that "free speech" has limitations in the Netherlands and especially so if you dare to criticize Muslims.

Now, as we watch with horror the savagery and barbarism of millions of Muslims in the Middle East and beyond the western world will continue to deny that it has anything to do with Islam. Barack Obama said that the beheading of Jim Foley had nothing to do with a religious system and yet in the name of Islam we have witnessed little five year old girls being sawn in half and beheaded and thousands of Christians and other religious groups have been crucified, murdered and chased from their homes. This is happening all over the world in the name of Islam and yet no one will call it out for what it is. Indeed, on the contrary, western leaders have expressed dismay that their nationals are perpetrating these hideous crimes and possibly going to return home to their countries, in significant numbers, to wage violent jihad against them.

Actually, all of this is not surprising as many well respected commentators saw it all coming and sounded the alarm only to be laughed at, smeared as bigots and ignored. They were accused of being guilty of Islamaphobia and consequently written off as extremists. Sadly, the confirming measure of this evil is the rise of anti-Semitism in Europe and now in America. Jews are now fair game and so they walk the streets of Paris, Malmo, Amsterdam, Brussels and London in fear of being verbally assaulted and even physically assaulted. In some countries like France, where liberty, freedom and equality became the watch words, Jews are now being murdered by Muslims. The Jews of Malmo in Sweden have been driven out for the same reasons and in Germany, just seventy odd years after the Second World War, the cries of "Juden Shies" (*Sh-t*), "Juden Shwien" and "Death to the Jews" have been heard again on the streets of Berlin, Munich and Stuttgart. As usual the politicians wring their hands in dismay as if it were all unexpected but nothing will change except the onward march toward the destruction of a civilization that was made great and became the admiration of the world because of its Judeo-Christian under pinning's.

Given the vast and growing Muslim communities in their backyards these western governments can no longer stand up for what is right and what is wrong. They have lost their moral compass because they gleefully rejected their foundations and therefore, like Esau, they will lose their inheritance. The last war between Hamas and Israel clearly demonstrated this. Israel was clearly attacked by a barbaric enemy that by its own confession and charter is dedicated to Israel's destruction. They have no interest in a "two-state" solution or in peaceful coexistence but rather in the annihilation of Israel and the murder of every Jew on the planet. These are their self confessed goals so one would think that the western world would fully back Israel. No, you would have to think again as the western media did its very best to discredit Israel and their spineless politicians, knowing full well that Israel is morally right and entitled to vigorously defend itself, jumped on the band wagon of accusing Israel of war crimes because civilians were killed in facilities from which Hamas fighters were launching missiles. This is not speculation but established truth; even United Nation's schools and clinics were utilized in this way! The hypocrisy of all this is indeed breathtaking but it stems from the abandonment of a proper moral compass which leads to foolishness.

Sadly it will not deter these western leaders because, if the truth be made known, they are scared to death of the Muslim backlash that will erupt in their cities if they do what is right and therefore stand resolutely with Israel. We are indeed watching the collapse of western civilization.

In the end Israel will stand alone, as it always has, but not entirely alone as her God will arise from the veiled shadows and defend her even though all nations may abandon her and come against her. The great Hebrew Prophet spoke of such a day and it will certainly come to pass; I fear sooner than we think.

> **"And it shall happen in that day that I will make Jerusalem a very heavy stone for all peoples; all who would heave it away will surely be cut in pieces, though all nations of the earth are gathered against it."**

> **"In that day the Lord will defend the inhabitants of Jerusalem; the one who is feeble among them in that day shall be like David, and the house of David shall be like God, like the Angel of the Lord before them. It shall be in that day I will seek to destroy all the nations that come against Jerusalem."**

> **Zechariah 12:3; 8-9**

Our modern western leaders forget that it was upon this Bible that its Kings and Queens were crowned and in great and beautiful places of Christian worship this glorious book, its saving message and its Savior Jesus were honored and glorified. Gifted and great preachers brought hope and light to millions and consequently the manners of society, the schools, hospitals and the penal institutions and houses of governance were reformed and so the people were given hope as their world enjoyed the blessings that the Judeo-Christian world brought to them. Not so any longer; things are about to change and dramatically so! Who cares?

HABAKKUK

"Though the fig tree may not blossom, nor fruit be on the vines; though the labor of the olive may fail, and the fields yield no food; though the flock may be cut off from the fold, and there be no herd in the stalls-Yet I will rejoice in the Lord, I will joy in the God of my salvation. The Lord God is my strength; He will make my feet like deer's feet, and He will make me walk on my high hills."

Habakkuk 3:17-19

Habakkuk is another pre-exilic prophet sent by God to the nation of Judah. He is filled with questions about God's dealings with his people just as we are filled with questions about God's acts in history. Consequently he is given a lesson in the sovereignty of God that we would do well to learn. Most of all he teaches us that when the righteous are caught up into the troubles of the ungodly they can survive by their faith and still enjoy a rich and satisfying spiritual life. Peter affirmed that God is well able to save the righteous from temptations and troubles:

"...then the Lord knows how to deliver the godly out of temptations and to reserve the unjust under punishment for the day of judgment."

2 Peter 2:9

The Prophet's questions and God's answers (1:1-4; 5-11; 12-17)

> "Why do You show me iniquity, and cause me to see
> trouble? For plundering and violence are before me;
> there is strife, and contention arises. Therefore the
> law is powerless, and justice never goes forth. For the
> wicked surround the righteous; therefore perverse
> judgment proceeds."

> **Habakkuk 1:3-4**

Habakkuk is alarmed by the state of the nation and he is also intimidated by the growth of ungodliness. He wonders why he, as a righteous man, has to put up with such wickedness and why God does not intervene to stop it all? We all have such questions since we know that God can do anything and therefore, in our thinking, He should put a stop to all the ungodliness around us. But God is just and righteous and the prophet has to learn that He must do justly in all the earth and therefore, in the dispensing of justice, He has a big surprise in store for Habakkuk. That is, Habakkuk is going to have to see even more wickedness in that God is calling for a very wicked nation to be the instrument of His judgment when dispensing justice to Judah. Habakkuk will be "utterly astounded" *(V5)* and indeed he was.

> "For indeed I am raising up the Chaldeans, a bitter and
> hasty nation which marches through the breadth of
> the earth, to possess dwelling places that are not theirs.
> They are terrible and dreadful."

> **Habakkuk 1:6**

The Babylonians will be called by God from the north east to invade Judah, lay siege to Jerusalem and ultimately destroy the city with its beloved Temple *(V6-7)*. They will be violent beyond anything that Habakkuk has ever seen and of course they will attribute their success to their gods *(V11)*. Habakkuk can't bear to hear this news as he was hoping that God would step in "privately as it were" to sort out Judah's problems and the thought that a gentile nation, serving dirty gods, would be the chosen instrument of God to judge and humble his people is shocking indeed. Consequently he cries out, "You cannot do this!" The truth is God can and did.

> **"Are You not from everlasting, O Lord my God, my Holy One? We shall not die. O Lord you have appointed them for judgment; O Rock you have marked them for correction. You are of purer eyes than to behold evil, and cannot look on wickedness. Why do you look on those who deal treacherously, and hold Your tongue when the wicked devours a person more righteous than he?"**   **Habakkuk 1:12-13**

The Second World War was a lesson in God using Hitler and His evil hordes to judge Europe and indeed Britain for their ungodliness. In the end God destroyed the wickedness and evil of the Third Reich but not before He had meted out His correction on the nations. I fear for America and even the West as we see unbridled wickedness, blasphemy and paganism taking root in these nations again. Truly God is not mocked and He has warned that He will yet again make a "full end of the nations" *(Jeremiah 30:11)*. His instruments in this regard will be astonishing and they will serve false gods and humiliate us *(Daniel 11:36-39)*. We have been warned by Habakkuk.

The prophet then argues with God and tells Him that "You are of purer eyes than to behold evil, and cannot look on wickedness. Why do You look on those who deal treacherously, and hold your tongue when the wicked devours a person more righteous than he?" *(V13)*. God is undeterred and He will bring forth His instrument of judgment that He calls "His servant" in Jeremiah's prophecy *(Jeremiah 25:9)*. Habakkuk rests his case and waits for God's answer again to his question.

The Prophet's position and God's answer (2:1; 2-20)

> **"Behold the proud; his soul is not upright in him; but the just shall live by his faith."**   **Habakkuk 2:4**

Habakkuk decides to wait on God through prayer that he may ultimately hear the voice of God and thereby prepare for all that is to come. This is a wise decision indeed. Prayer is our only real place of refuge and it is a very special place and gift whereby God can draw us to Himself, give us discernment and impart wisdom to us. We need to pray more and sadly the modern church everywhere has all but abandoned the place of prayer. Our churches may throng with people but the prayer meeting remains badly attended, weak and without real direction and urgency. The enemy is really at the door and no one is sounding the alarm. Jesus said that we are to watch and pray and He also questioned whether he would find prayer on the earth in the days leading up to His second coming.(*Luke 18:8*). It's as if He knew that we would abandon prayer in favor of "good meetings." Subsequently the "glory has departed" and all the while darkness closes in. Habakkuk teaches us that prayer is the single and most important activity that we can and should regularly engage in.

God's answer comes and the prophet is told to write it down because, "it will not lie. Though it tarries, wait for it; because it will surely come." The Babylonians will come and judge Judah; this is certain and the vision will be fulfilled. The remnant and faithful people of God, in right standing with God, will have to walk with Him by faith alone. Their faith will see them through, for by it God will be with them and save them. This of course was the great clarion call of the Reformation and it constitutes the only way to be saved. We have to exercise living faith in all that God, by Jesus Christ, has done for us on the cross. We have to begin by faith, live by faith and stand in faith. There is just no other way to please God. Paul wrote:

> **"For by grace you have been saved through faith, and that not of yourselves; it is the gift of God."**
> **Ephesians 2:8**

> **"Knowing that a man is not justified by the works of the Law but by faith in Jesus Christ, even we have believed in Christ Jesus, that we might be justified by faith and not by the works of the law..."**
>
> **Galatians 2:16**

> **"But without faith it is impossible to please Him, for he who comes to God must believe that He is, and that He is a rewarder of those who diligently seek Him."**
>
> **Hebrews 11:6**

God is about to judge Judah for countless manifestations of wickedness and He lists these by saying firstly woe; meaning be alarmed and afraid. He thus says:

Woe to the profiteers and racketeers who accumulate wealth at the expense of others (*V6-8*).

Woe to the rich who have fine houses but hate God and think that their houses will protect them *(V9-11)*.

Woe to those who build communities and set up principles whereby they reject God *(V12-14)*. They are fools because they cannot hold back the knowledge of the Lord because one day the earth will be filled with it "as the waters cover the sea" *(V14)*.

Woe to him who encourages drunkenness *(V15-16)*. Indeed the Lord's wine cup of judgment will be poured out upon him.

Woe to those who worship idols *(V18-19)*. An idol is anything in your life that is more important than God. It could be a hobby, one's profession or even one's children. If these hold a greater place in our lives than Jesus then we are idolaters!

A casual reading of these "woes" will reveal that our cities, nations, communities and even churches are filled with them. Consequently God is in His holy Temple and eventually He will come forth in judgment. Habakkuk has received his answer and so now he must wait patiently with God for that day to come. John's Revelation also contains a list of "woes" that will shortly befall the earth.

> **"And I looked, and I heard an angel flying through the midst of heaven, saying with a loud voice. "Woe, woe, woe to the inhabitants of the earth, becauseof the remaining blasts of the trumpet of the three angels who are about to sound."**

> **Revelation 8:13**

The Prophets prayer (3:1-16)

> **"O lord, I have heard your speech and was afraid; O Lord, revive Your work in the midst of the years! In the midst of the years make it known; in wrath remember mercy."**

> **Habakkuk 3:2**

Habakkuk knows that the only hope is that the true people of God begin to call on God and that His work be revived amongst them. Revival alone will save the nation and so he pleads for a visitation from heaven that will bring renewal and avert a disaster. "In wrath remember mercy" he cries out and we should learn from him that there is still hope if only God's people everywhere would wake up and call on God. We need another Wesleyan revival! Habakkuk then launches into a eulogy of praise that reflects the fact that he has finally got the message and he has come to understand why God must be true to His character and bring judgment on the nation. His eulogy recognizes God's greatness in creation and that He is everlasting with great power and has done great things for Israel. He even stopped the sun and the moon in order to save and help Israel and He vanquished her enemies by making "the waters a heap"; a reference to the deliverance from Egypt. A God who has done so many great things for His people is just and righteous when He rides forth to judge them because of their sin and rejection of Him. He thus ends his great prayer by saying:

> **"When I heard, my body trembled; my lips quivered at the voice; rottenness entered my bones; and I trembled in myself, that I might rest in the day of trouble. When he comes up to the people, he will invade them with his troops."**

> **Habakkuk 3:16**

The Prophets Hymn of praise (3:17-19)

> **"The Lord is my strength; He will make my feet like deer's feet, and He will make me walk on my high hills."**

> **Habakkuk 3:19**

Habakkuk is now finally at peace because he recognizes that nothing, not even the invading Babylonian army can rob him of his blessed destiny in God. God has "high hills" just for him because he has remained faithful and true in his commitment to Him. Outward circumstances, though dire, cannot rob him of his joy and blessing because God is his salvation and strength and nothing in heaven or earth can change that. He will thus joy in the God of His salvation and, like a mountain deer in the Negev wilderness, he will ascend to heights unknown and there walk in new ways with God even though all around him is calamity and disaster.

Have you learned this lesson? It is an important one. Here ends Habakkuk's prophetic message.

DEVOTION

Law and Grace

"For the Law was given through Moses, but grace And truth came through Jesus Christ."

John 1:17

The Prophet Habakkuk reminds us that the "just shall live by faith." It was this truth that sparked Luther's Reformation and returned the people of God to the biblical idea of God's grace as the grounds of our salvation. This is certainly true and must be defended rigorously but we still need to know where the Law fits in to this scheme of things. That is, the Church has never adequately dealt with the relationship between Law and Grace in the Bible. If anything Christians tend to write off the Law as being irrelevant but, by contrast, Jesus said that anyone who diminishes the importance and significance of the Law will be called "least in the Kingdom of heaven" (*Matthew 5:19*). Paul reminds us that Jesus died on the cross in order that the requirement of the Law may be fulfilled in us (*Romans 8:3-4*)! What then does all this mean?

1. **Definition and nature of the Law** The Law or Torah of God can be divided into three parts. That is, the Civil Law, the Ceremonial or Liturgical Law and the Moral or Majestic Law. The Civil Law deals with the regulation of social or national life and so concentrates on disease control, behavior, the dispensing of justice and taxation etc. The Ceremonial Law is embodied in the sacrificial system and Temple ritual and the Majestic or Moral Law constitutes the demands of God's character. It is a written

description of His glory and is thus chiefly contained in what we call the Ten Commandments. We sin when we break this code of conduct *(Romans 3:23)*. It is to be noted that the Civil Law and the Ceremonial Law have both been abolished *(Hebrews 8:13)*.

The Moral Law When Paul writes about the Law in the New Testament he is in fact writing about the Moral Law or Ten Commandments. This Law is good, spiritual and if perfectly kept will impart eternal life *(Romans 7:10; 12)*! Jesus Himself expounded this Law in Matthew five, six and seven and warned that heaven and earth would pass away before its significance and importance would *(Matthew 5:17-18)*. We would do well to take note of this. Of course no one can or ever has, except for Jesus, kept this Law. We have all failed in this regard and so this Law also becomes our teacher. That is, when preached it confirms that we are law breakers or sinners; thus guilty before God and subject to the penalty of eternal death *(Romans 3:23; Romans 3:19-20; Galatians 3:24; Romans 6:23)*. In short the Law becomes our enemy, though it is good and spiritual, and it condemns and places us under the wrath of God *(Romans 8:21-24)*. In other words, there is no one who can be justified before God by trying to keep it *(Acts 13:39)*. It is because of this negative function of the Law that Christians tend to write it off! It should be noted that Gospel preaching that excludes it is false because such preaching will not convict of sin and lead people to repentance. Only by the Law does the knowledge of sin come to our hearts and we are to repent of our sins in order to be saved! The Psalmist tell us that the Law is good because it converts the soul and leads it to repentance *(Psalm 19:7)*. In fact God commands us to repent *(John 16:8; Acts 17:30; Luke 24:46-47)*. This was at the very heart of the preaching of John and Charles Wesley and it was precisely why they were called "people of the method" and so Methodists.

2. **The New Covenant** The goal of the New Covenant is to get this Majestic Law, in the person of Jesus, into our hearts. Please read Jeremiah 31:31-34 and Hebrews 8:7-13. Also Paul teaches us that the purpose of Jesus' death was to bring us to a place where this Law is fulfilled in us spontaneously and with joy as we walk

in the Spirit *(Romans 8:3-4)*. The gift of eternal life is the Moral Law embodied in the person of Jesus living in our hearts *(Romans 6:22-23)*! It is only His finished work on the cross that makes all of this possible. For this reason He teaches us, by expounding the Moral Law, as recorded in Matthew five, what "born again living" looks like. We would do well to note this. Jesus' death on the cross frees us forever from the condemnation of the Law; it meets all the Law's requirements on our behalf and is all sufficient in that in encompasses the behavior of our entire lives. This is what we mean by grace, but not cheap grace as it has come to us at a huge price. God died for us (1Corinthians 6:20)! We who receive such grace hate sin and do not "play" with it but when we sin we have an Advocate Who will cleanse us from all unrighteousness (Jude 20-23) (1John 1:8-9). It is worth noting that in the Hebrew the words "New Covenant" really mean "a Restored or Renewed Covenant." That is, the New Covenant, ratified by Jesus' spilt blood, is the power or ability of the Law. What was good and spiritual but weakened by our flesh has now been given ability through Christ. This is precisely why John's Gospel opens with the statement, "The Law was given through Moses but grace and truth came through Jesus Christ." Jesus didn't abandon the Law, He fulfilled it perfectly, in His life, and then in ours by His presence, but this was made possible only by His death!

3. **The Construction of the Bible** An alternative way to understand our Bibles, if we are ever going to reach the Jewish world, would be to see its composition thus:
    The Five Books of Moses-The giving of the Law
    Joshua, Judges, Kings, Chronicles etc-The history of the Law
    Psalms, Proverbs, Ecclesiastes etc-The rejoicing over the Law
    The Major and Minor Prophets- A commentary on Israel's obedience and disobedience to the Law
    The Four Gospels-The ability of the Law
    The Acts of the Apostles-The spreading of the Law
    The Epistles-The inward nature and presence of the Law
    The Revelation- The triumph of the Law

It is interesting to note that when Jesus comes again and sets up His earthly Kingdom the Moral Law will be the foundation of His global kingdom *(Isaiah*

2:1-4). It is also worth noting that the longest "chapter" in the Bible is Psalm 119. This amazing Psalm is all about the importance of God's Majestic Law and constitutes a call to live one's life by it. This is especially important when one considers that the instrument of God's judgment, by which the world will be held accountable, will be the Law *(Romans 2:12-16)*. We thank God for Jesus Who has, by His cross, made possible our joyful and spontaneous obedience to the Law *(Romans 8:3-4)*. Blessed be His name!

NAHUM

"Behold, on the mountains the feet of him who brings good tidings, who proclaims peace! O Judah, keep your appointed feasts, perform your vows. For the wicked one shall no more pass through you; he is utterly cut off."

Nahum 1:15

Judah's existence was constantly being threatened by Nineveh the capital of the Assyrian Empire and embodiment of it. The northern kingdom of Israel had already been ravaged, plundered and exiled by the Assyrians in 722 BC and now Nineveh was poised to strike deeper south. In many respects the threat that Nineveh posed to Judah served, under God, as a reminder that Judah would be judged if she abandoned and sinned against Him. Indeed, because of God's love for Nineveh, a city of one hundred and twenty thousand people (*Jonah 4:11*), He had already sent them the Prophet Jonah whose epic voyage, deliverance from the belly of the whale and highly successful evangelistic mission is recorded in the biblical book bearing his name. Under Jonah's preaching Nineveh had repented of its wickedness and had turned to God. He, formerly breathing destruction against the city, relented and instead visited her with grace and mercy.

However, with the passing of time Nineveh forgot the goodness of God, returned to her old wicked ways and attracted thereby the judgment of God. Nahum is the chosen instrument by which this warning of impending judgment is delivered to the city. Truly Nineveh has become the enemy of God and so the book opens with these words:

> **"God is jealous, and the Lord avenges; the Lord will take vengeance on His adversaries, and He reserves wrath for His enemies; the Lord is slow to anger and great in power, and will not at all acquit the wicked."**
>
> **Nahum 1:2-3**

The book of Nahum, like the other Mini Prophets:

Reminds us of the sovereignty of God (1:2-14)

Here we are given a majestic view of God's sovereignty that is summed up in ways that we can easily relate to. This great God of the Bible can control the winds, clouds and seas and the very earth heaves and shakes at His presence. No one can stand up to Him or against Him. Moreover, His great sovereignty is always attached to His righteousness and justice and therefore He will always look with favor upon those who trust in Him faithfully. So, Nahum writes:

> **"The Lord is good, a stronghold in the day of trouble; and He knows those who trust in Him."**
>
> **Nahum 1:7**

We clearly learn from this:

1. That God loves Gentile peoples and always did. He looked down on Nineveh and recognized that within its walls were men and women who still trusted in Him. For them He would be a stronghold in the day of trouble. A reminder that our spiritual and physical well being is not determined by external events around us but by our relationship with God.
2. That God engages nations and will dictate their rise and fall *(Daniel 2:21)* according to their levels of righteousness and wickedness. Solomon wrote that, "Righteousness exalts a nation but sin is a disgrace to any people" *(Proverbs 14:34)*.
3. That God loves cities. He had in fact sent Jonah to Nineveh because he cared about the people; even their animals *(Jonah 4:11)*.
4. That God hates wickedness, especially drunkenness because it further ravages the image of God and turns people into brute beasts *(1:10)*.

Reminds us that Israel's existence is linked to the Gospel of Jesus *(1:15)*

> **"Behold, on the mountains the feet of him who brings good tidings, who proclaims peace!"**

So, here again, Nahum, like his fellow prophets sees into the future and tells Judah that her peace-real peace- is only found in her acceptance of Jesus' message of good news. Paul affirms this in Romans where he writes, "How beautiful are the feet of those who preach the gospel of peace, who bring glad tidings of good things," *(Romans 10:15)*. Indeed Jesus Himself said this when He wept over Jerusalem:

> **"Now as He drew near, He saw the city and wept over it, saying, "If you had known, even you, especially in this your day, the things that make for your peace! but now they are hidden from your eyes."**
>
> **Luke 19:41-42**

Consequently for near on 2000 years peace has alluded the Jewish people because they missed "their day", have been blind to who Jesus really is; but it will all change. In reality then, the drama and conflict unfolding in Israel and the Middle East today will only come to an end when Israel finally accepts the "feet of Him who brings good news."

Reminds us that a glorious restoration awaits Judah *(2:1-12)*

These verses should be read in conjunction with the one above, that is with verse fifteen of chapter one. The truth to underline is; that a restoration process in Israel will not be complete without a restoration to the Lord. This process of restoration is now unfolding before our eyes and it is twofold in nature: First a restoration to the land and then, secondly, a restoration to the Lord. The Major Prophets speak of it and so Ezekiel writes:

> **"For I will take you from among the nations, gather you out of all countries, and bring you into your own land. Then I will sprinkle clean water on you, and you shall be clean; I will cleanse you from all your filthiness and from all your idols. I will give you a new heart and put a new spirit within you; I will take the heart of stone out of your flesh and give you a heart of flesh."**
>
> **Ezekiel 36:24-26**

Peter also preached about it after he and John, in Jesus' name, raised the lame man at the gates of the Temple. He said that Jesus would stay in heaven until *"the restoration of all things"* would unfold in Israel *(Acts 3:16-21)*. Nahum sees this glorious day and refers to it in this way:

"For the Lord will restore the excellence of Jacob like the excellence of Israel...."   **Nahum 2:2**

So then the issue of the "tidings of good news" is the one that is to dominate our prayers and intercession for Israel today. There will be no full restoration in Zion and until the good news of Jesus is restored to the people. In other words, the present conflict will continue to rage until Israel finally recognizes Jesus' messianic credentials.

Reminds us that God does not relent *(2:3-13)*

Here we have a record of God's unrelenting anger against Nineveh. She has crossed a line and will now be brought down and all their faces will be drained of color *(2:10)*. Terror will grip Nineveh as a new empire lays her waste and plunders her unbridled wealth. The Babylonians are on the rise and they will savage Nineveh as she has savaged others, including the northern kingdom of Israel. The heavenly decree is unalterable:

> **"Behold, "I am against you," says the Lord of hosts, I will burn your chariots in smoke, and the sword shall devour your young lions; I will cut off your prey from the earth, and your messengers shall be heard no more."**
>
> **Nahum 2:13**

Nineveh fell just as God had warned and she has passed into history as mere sand and stubble; a testimony to the veracity of God's word. Indeed if God is against you as a nation you have no hope and a huge problem. The book of Revelation asserts that God has a problem with most of the cities of the world and consequently they too will fall just as Nineveh did. This should drive us to the place of prayer and to make every effort to reach our cities with the Gospel of Jesus before it is too late.

> **"Now the great city was divided into three parts, and the cities of the nations fell. And great Babylon was remembered before God to give her the cup of the wine of the fierceness of His wrath."**
>
> **Revelation 16:19**

Reminds us that God will have the last say about our cities *(3:1-19)*
Nahum ends his oracle with an in depth description of the fall of Nineveh. He writes that God will, "cast abominable filth upon you" and that the terror will be so severe that the once proud soldiers of Nineveh will be like women *(3:13)*. All of this wakes us up to the fact that ultimately God raises up cities, leaders and nations and it is He who gives them honor and prestige and who will tear them down. Even our democratic systems are "manipulated" by Him to set in place the leaders that we truly deserve. This is a fearful thing because it tells us that the spiritual state of nations before God determines what sort of governments they will get. No wonder Paul exhorted the church of his day to place leaders of cities and nations at the very top of its prayer list.

> **"Therefore I exhort first of all that supplications, prayers, intercessions, and giving of thanks be made for all men, for kings and all who are in authority, that we may lead a quiet and peaceable life in all godliness and reverence."** 1 Timothy 2:1-2

Certainly the book of Revelation gives us a warning of what is to come in chapter eighteen of this important oracle. We should read it carefully and make sure that our lives are not entangled with the wickedness of the city but are by contrast a reflection of the righteousness and justice of Jesus. We should then be in the city but not of it and this is precisely why John calls us to come out of her because God is going to overthrow her.

> **"The kings of the earth who committed fornication and lived luxuriously with her will weep and lament for her, when they see the smoke of her burning, standing at a distance for fear of her torment, saying, 'Alas, alas, that great city Babylon, that mighty city! For in one hour your judgment has come."**
>
> **Revelation 18:9-10**

> **"And I heard another voice from heaven saying, "Come out of her, my people, lest you share in her sins, and lest you receive her plagues. For her sins have reached to heaven, and God has remembered her iniquities."**
>
> **Revelation 18:4-5**

So ends Nahum's prophetic vision; it does not end in hope. Nineveh will fall and did! Death and destruction became her lot and her end was terrible. Nahum, like all the Mini Prophets, brings our attention to the phenomenon of the judgment of God; a subject not popular in pulpits today but one that will help us understand God's character, His ways and what He requires from us. We must fear God more, walk humbly before Him and live lives that please Him. Above all we must be His voice in the world, as Nahum was, since we have a message that extends His love, grace and mercy to those who will hear it.

Also, Nahum reminds us that God's people get caught up in the upheavals that befall nations. Christians fought on both sides of the battle lines in the First and Second World Wars and God took note and cared for them. This is His promise by the voice of His servant Nahum.

DEVOTION

Jesus is Greater

Therefore, holy brethren, partakers of the heavenly calling, consider the Apostle and High Priest of our confession, Christ Jesus, who was faithful to Him who appointed Him, as Moses also was faithful in all His house. For this One has been counted worthy of more glory that Moses, inasmuch as He who built the house has more honor than the house. For every house is built by someone, but He who built all things is God. And Moses indeed was faithful in all His house as a servant, for a testimony of those things which would be spoken of afterward, but Christ as a Son over His own house, whose house we are if we hold fast the confidence and the rejoicing of the hope firm to the end."
Hebrews 3:1-6

The Prophet Nahum reminds us that the answer for Israel and indeed the whole world is the good news of Jesus. This good news is brought to the world by preachers who have themselves been touched and transformed by it. Nahum with his focus on the city of Nineveh teaches us that God cares about cities and what happens to their inhabitants. They need deliverance from their sins and only the proclamation of the Gospel will do this. Israel too needs to receive "the feet of them that bring tidings of good news" but they must be convinced that the author of this good news is greater than Moses.

The Book of Hebrews is written to Jewish believers who were tempted, because of peer pressure and persecution, to abandon their faith in Christ. The writer of the book is determined to encourage them and he does so by placing before them the greatness of Jesus. Indeed he opens the book with the startling notion that Jesus is the very Creator and the outshining of all that God is. In short, Jesus is God! He then augments this argument by demonstrating that Jesus is God because He is greater than Angels, because the testimony of scripture affirms this and because He is far greater than Moses, the revered Law Giver of Israel. This one of a kind Godman died for our sins and thereby released us from the tyranny of death, delivered us from all demonic power and reconciled us to God, His Father.

The main body of the book, however, sets out to prove that Jesus is greater than Moses and that His work on the cross is a fulfillment of Moses' work, which by the wilderness tabernacle, was only a picture, though a very glorious one, of all that Jesus, would come and do. Moses thus dealt only with pictures and shadows but Jesus entered the more perfect tabernacle of God's real presence in heaven and there presented His blood as an atonement for the world's sins. Moses is therefore great, indeed very great, but Jesus is greater! Jesus' work was real; Moses' work was preparatory by nature and therefore only a shadow of the good things to come in Christ. Or, to put it in the writer's own words: Moses faithfully served God in His House but Jesus built the real House of God by the spilling of His blood by virtue of His indestructible life. Jesus is, therefore, greater than Moses and should be listened to because we shall not escape if we neglect the great salvation that Moses only pictured but which Jesus accomplished on the cross.

The writer then reminds his readers that great spiritual truths can be neglected and lost because we are weak and prone to drift. So, often it is not deliberate rebellion that takes us away from Christ but neglect and sheer spiritual laziness. Open rebellion will however leave us in a dangerous place as it could so offend God that He will not take us back even if we cry out for it. This is no idle warning. The greatness of Jesus is overwhelming and we must retain it before our spiritual eyes by not growing weary but by looking unto Him every day because He is the author and finisher of our faith. There is no trial or difficulty that should dissuade us from staying true to Him and we must learn to endure all of these because the prize of gaining His glory is worth it all. Jesus is greater!

Moreover, retaining Jesus' greatness in our lives means that we should recognize that His life is given to us through the shared experience of gathering together to worship Him. We must then not neglect our "assembling together", we must encourage each other as we see the day of His second coming drawing nearer, we must submit to godly leaders, we must draw near to God by regular devotion and we must "consider one another in order to stir up love and good works."

Moses was indeed a very great man. He led over one million people out of Egypt into a wilderness and by the outstretched hand of God, fed them, delivered them, protected them and organized them into a great nation under God. Jesus, by contrast, has led billions out of the Egypt of sin and has brought them into the very near presence of God. Moses brought his people to a mountain that thundered, smoked and shook with lightning bolts thus striking fear into the hearts of his people, but Jesus has led His people into the very near and loving embrace of God. He is just greater!